THE CHRISTIAN
HOME SCHOOL

THE CHRISTIAN HOME SCHOOL

Gregg Harris

Noble Publishing Associates
Gresham, Oregon

NOBLE PUBLISHING ASSOCIATES
P.O. Box 2250
Gresham, Oregon 97030

First printing, January 1988.
Second printing, March 1988
Third printing, July 1995

Printed in the United States of America

ISBN 1-56857-025-2

9 791568 570258

To my wife
Sono
and my children
Joshua, Joel, Alex, Brett, Sarah and Isaac
(Philippians 1:9-11)

CONTENTS

ACKNOWLEDGEMENTS

This book is born of my acquaintance with countless alumni and friends of *The Home Schooling Workshop*. Their life experiences, added to and seen through my own, have added a depth of practicality which would not otherwise have been possible. For their willingness to answer my queries and share their adventures in Christian home schooling, I am most grateful.

America is the best half-educated country in the world.
Nicholas Murray Butler

AN ADVENTURE OF FAITH AND LEARNING

It's been a long while since very many of us took the issue of education seriously. We have been paying our taxes and assuming the schools are doing an adequate job. But that had best change. Quickly.

It's not that the educational system in the United States has completely failed. It has, in fact, enjoyed some limited success. It's just that many of these successes have been in all the wrong areas. It has successfully produced a nation with massive adult illiteracy. It has successfully broken the moral backbone of our youth. It has successfully and subtly undermined parental authority. It has weakened the confidence of America in the free market system. It has successfully made us, as the President's report on education asserted, "a nation at risk."

Clearly, the actual "successes" of the educational system make for a stark contrast with the successes educators have continually promised us since the inception of the public schools. In the middle of the last century, Horace Mann spoke of public education as man's greatest discovery, and of the local schools as the institutions that would ultimately usher in a "golden age." At the beginning of this century, John Dewey claimed that American education could be used to build a great "socialist utopia." But the proof is in the pudding. Johnny can't read. Susie can't spell. Willie can't write. Arthur can't add. And all four of them are caught in the awful web of promiscuity, rebellion, drug abuse, rootlessness, and violence.

Public educators have had their chance. And they've failed the test.

In response to the "successes" of the public educational system, hundreds of thousands of parents have discovered an alternative. Their children aren't going to school anymore. They *are* being educated, though. They're just not *going* to school; they're staying home to be taught by their own parents.

Now, that may be a terribly alien concept for you. School at home? If you're not actually a home schooler yourself, you probably have some serious questions about those who are. Are the kids really learning? Are the parents really qualified to teach? Are these folks just a group of religious fanatics out on the fringe? Why are their ranks growing so dramatically? Why would parents want to spend *so much* of their time with their children? Is it even legal? And what about socialization? Will these children grow up to be nerds?

Perhaps some of your neighbors home school their children, and you are wondering what goes on behind their doors. Why not ask them? You will probably be pleasantly surprised. In the meantime, read on. I've heard almost every imaginable objection to home schooling, and I believe there are good answers to each of them. This book is an attempt to profile those answers in a practical, easy-to-grasp fashion.

But before we dig in and provide those answers, here is the bottom line: *most home-schooling parents are Christians who are returning to home schooling because they have come to grips with their God-given responsibility to provide their children's education.*

Notice: I have chosen two of those words—*returning* and *responsibility*—very carefully.

Parents are *returning* to home schooling. The practice of home schooling is nothing new; not in our culture, and certainly not in other cultures throughout the world. It is the most ancient and time-honored method of educating children. Public education, on the other hand, is a new idea. Begun in this country nearly one hundred years ago, in 1837, as a tax-supported experiment, public education is utterly and completely unprecedented and unproven. The warnings of its earliest critics have all come true. And except for its perpetual cycle of tax reform, its party would long since be over. So, home schooling is simply a *return* to the educational system that made this nation and every other nation great. It is a return to the system of family study and instruction that gave us such leaders as George Washington, Abraham Lincoln, Robert E. Lee, Oliver Wendell Holmes, Theodore Roosevelt, Booker T. Washington and Harry Truman.

But, understand, modern home schooling is not mere nostalgia. It is not simply a return to *tradition* for the sake of *traditionalism*. The home school movement is using the latest technology to provide an old-fashioned, high-quality education. Most home-schooling parents also come to grips with their God-given *responsibility* to oversee their children's education. They know that God has given them an awesome stewardship over their children for a *very* short while. And they must make the most of it. They must raise up those children "in the discipline and instruction of the Lord" (Ephesians 6:4). Practically, that means they don't simply have a *right* to supervise the education of their children, they have a *duty*. A person can occasionally waive his rights, but never his duties.

Perhaps you already know all these things, and you have decided to home school your own children. This book will encourage you to follow through. It will tell you how to get started and point you in the right direction, once you're on your way. It will answer many of your "who," "what," "when," "where," "how," and "Why" questions.

On the other hand, maybe you're not considering home schooling your children, but you're curious about those who do. You may be a pastor, a lawyer, a public school administrator, a teacher, or a grandparent who wants to better understand Christian home-schooling families. I invite you to read on. Find out why home schooling is the most exciting and fastest growing Christian educational movement in our nation today. Then lend a hand in making it even better.

Join us in this adventure of faith and learning!

The fate of empires depends on the education of youth.
Aristotle

OUR CHILDREN, OUR FUTURE

Several years ago, a group of parents in Dallas came together to discuss a few common concerns. Their children, they had observed, were being negatively influenced by ideas they were bringing home day by day—ideas which were quite foreign to their own values and perspective. These parents were frustrated and were finding it increasingly difficult to pass on the distinctives of their faith to their children, who were spending most of their waking hours behind public school desks. Realizing what had to be done, they proceeded to take the appropriate action.

The parents took their children out of the public schools. But did they want their children to grow up as devout illiterates? Absolutely not. They promptly started their own school—a parent-supervised, parent-taught school—which better suited their purpose and principles.

This action marked a first in Dallas.

The great city in the buckle of the Bible Belt saw its first private *Moslem* school!

The new school satisfied those parents who thought it simply wasn't possible for Moslem children in the public schools to get an education from an Islamic perspective. Consider what worked against them. Most of their classmates weren't Moslem. None of their teachers were Moslem. And the curriculum certainly wasn't Moslem. It stood to reason that, if they wanted an education consistent with their religion, they'd have to provide it themselves. So they did.

Those parents had understood the reality of University of Chicago Professor Allan Bloom's arguments in his best-seller, *The Closing of the American Mind:*

"Every educational system has a moral goal that it tries to attain and that informs its curriculum. It wants to produce a certain kind of human being. Democratic education, whether it admits it or not, wants and needs to produce men and women who have the tastes, knowledge, and character supportive of a democratic regime."

No one starts a school just to teach the three Rs. Every school has a moral or political agenda. The public schools had a different "moral goal" in mind than did the Moslem parents. The state desired a system that would produce men and women supportive of its "regime." The Moslem parents, on the other hand, desired an educational system which would produce men and women who had Islamic "tastes, knowledge, and character." Education has always been a battleground in the culture wars.

When those children walked out of the public school doors for the last time, they left behind a host of classmates, many of them Christians, sons and daughters of conservative, evangelical, Bible-believing parents. The Christian kids probably went home and told Mom and Dad about the Moslem kids who wouldn't be coming back.

"Yeah, I guess their parents thought the public school wasn't good for Moslem kids because it sort of—well, you know—undermines their convictions about their faith."

Some might say, "Oh my! How radical! Yanking kids out of a *free* education! What did they expect to be taught in our public schools? After all, America is a *Christian* nation."

No, it's not. It used to be more Biblical and God-fearing. But it is not a Christian nation as I understand the term "Christian." The public schools are not *Christian* schools.

Thankfully, many parents all across this land have realized that the public school education their children are getting is not really Christian at all. They are waking up to the fact that there is a war going on.

If This is War, Where is the Fighting?

The movement to private Christian schools among conservative evangelicals began in earnest during the early 1960s. Christian authors have written scores of books since—critiques of statist education, each insisting that there is a battle raging in America and that Christians are in the midst of this war. Even their titles show just how serious they are. Tim LaHaye gave us *The Battle for the Public Schools.* Samuel Blumenfeld wrote *The NEA: Trojan Horse in American Education.* Lynn Buzzard wrote *Schools: They Haven't Got a Prayer.* Rick Cizik gave us *The High Cost of Indifference.* Dr. James Dobson and Gary Bauer wrote *Children at Risk,* and Cathy Duffy wrote *Government Nannies.*

To many ears, all this has sounded a bit melodramatic, especially when the locus of the battle is supposed to be public school classrooms. When we think of "our" public schools, we think all-American: red, white, and blue; apple pie; I-pledge-allegiance. School spirit dies slowly. We have too many memories of the smell of new crayons, august portraits of Washington and Lincoln, and matronly women teachers. It is hard to imagine that, within those sacred environs, a battle rages. But that is what is happening. The evidence is compelling us to take action.

The enemy army has already made its intentions clear. One of its more articulate writers revealed those intentions in *The Humanist* magazine recently:

> I am convinced that the battle for humankind's future must be waged and won in the public school classroom by teachers who correctly perceive their role as the proselytizers of a new faith: a religion of humanity that recognizes and respects the spark of what theologians call divinity in every human being. Their teachers must embody the same selfless dedication as the most rabid fundamentalist preachers, for they will be ministers of another sort, utilizing a classroom instead of a pulpit to convey humanist values in whatever subject they teach, regardless of the educational level—preschool, day care, or large university. The classroom must, and will, become an arena of conflict between the old and the new—the rotting corpse of Christianity, together with all its adjacent evils and misery, and the new faith of humanism.[2]

This is a declaration of religious war. We are not over-reacting. We are simply taking our enemy at his word. He wants our children.

The growing number of Christian parents who have become aware of such intentions—either because they have heard the trumpet blast of evangelical leaders or because they have felt the bitter sting of the battle themselves—have been shocked into action. They have found themselves making the same kinds of decisions as those that the Moslem parents in Dallas found necessary.

Some have put their children into private Christian schools. Many others—more than one million—have begun teaching their children at home. And in the process they have discovered a higher quality of education: tutoring.

As one pastor has said, "The public schools have taken heavy losses because droves of the best and the brightest have left. More to the point, the *principled* and the *disciplined* have left. Public educators have become outraged."[3] When the best and the brightest start leaving the state system, the public educators see the handwriting on the wall. They fight back, in the media and in court.

The question is, are these Christian parents escapists? Are they merely running away? Or have they found something to run to; a better approach? What often starts in response to the public schools' weaknesses, ends up firmly built on the homes' strengths. But the battle is real, in any case.

The Real Struggle

The real conflict over education in America today isn't primarily within the four walls of a public school classroom; rather, it lies between two very different schools of thought, both having their own very different moral goals, both propagating their own distinctive world-view, both wanting to produce a very different kind of human being.

Public schools and Christian schools (whether home or private) are religious rivals. Their teachers hold rival views of God, man, the family, the state, law, sex, origins, the past, the present, and the future.

The real battle isn't *for* the public schools; we never had them. The battle is for our children.

Many evangelical Christians still find it hard to accept this. While Roman Catholics, Lutherans, and Episcopalians have turned to parochial schools, evangelicals have naively considered the public schools "their own." Amazingly, they continue to speak hopefully of salvaging them. But consider the two primary items on the agenda to save the public schools.

Public School Prayer. Christians have spent a lot of time and dollars on this point. And yet, it is a token issue. Should prayer ever be legalized, the kids won't be allowed to *mention* Christ in their petitions, let alone offer them in His name. Public school prayer would be constrained to meet the lowest common denominator of religion. Such praying is manifestly UNCHRISTIAN. Just ask Isaiah, Jeremiah, or Ezekiel. Or, better yet, ask Daniel. Why should Christian children pray silently to the unknown god of American civil religion? We already have the right to remain silent.

Creationism. Christians have yet to win a court case on creationism. And what if they were to win? The public school teachers would be able to discuss creationism, but only if they left out the Creator. Why? Because some Christians keep insisting that creationism should be taught neutrally, side by side with evolution. Here comes the unknown god again. The New Agers love this kind of creationism. It opens the door for their pseudoscience.

As well-intentioned as these Christian efforts are, they fail to grasp the full implications of state-controlled education. It has been a century-and-a-half since the first public school, established by Unitarian Horace Mann, began working for a *state-controlled* school system. Unlike many present-day Christians, some of our nineteenth-century evangelical forebears could foresee the results. Southern Presbyterian Robert Lewis Dabney (1820-1898), for example, had this to say about "our" public schools:

> But nearly all public men and divines declare that the State schools are the glory of America, that they are a finality, and in no event to be surrendered. And we have seen that their complete secularization is *logically inevitable.* Christians must prepare themselves, then, for the following results: All prayers, catechisms, and Bibles will ultimately be driven out of the schools.[4]

Dabney also knew that the effects of secularization in the classroom would reach far beyond the playground.

We are attempting, then, an absolute novelty. But may not the tree be already known by its fruits? State education among Americans tends to be entirely secularized. What is the result? Whence this general revolt from the Christian faith in this country, so full of churches, preachers, and a redundant Christian literature, so boastful of its Sabbaths and its evangelism? What has prepared so many for the dreary absurdities of materialism? He who notes the current of opinion sees that the wisest are full of misgivings as to the fruits of present methods.[5]

More than a century later, Dabney's words still ring true. Matters *have* worsened. And the wisest *remain* full of misgivings.

This has persuaded many Christian parents to take their children out of public schools. But has it been fear only? Or has it also been faith? Both are involved. For what reasonable fear has initiated, Biblical faith has commandeered. Home schooling is an act of faith and hope, as well as parental discretion.

Am I My Child's Keeper?

If I am my brother's keeper, would it not follow that I am also my child's keeper?

The Christian's answer *should* be obvious. But for many, it is not so obvious. Rather than training their children to be true disciples of Christ, who could have a real impact on the world as young adults, too many parents are sending them out of the home and neighborhood at a tender age to evangelize an overtly anti-Christian public school system. Would these parents send their little ones to evangelize the Sunday school program of a religious cult? It would only be for an hour or so each week. No? Then why send the same children to evangelize the parochial schools of Secular Humanism and the New Age Movement for five to six hours per day, five days a week?

The key to winning the lost to Christ is in knowing who we are in Christ and then proclaiming the Gospel to others with that confidence. We serve from a position of inner strength. If, as Christ said, a student will become like his teacher (Luke 6:40), we are foolish to send children in to do a job that many adults seem ill-equipped to accomplish. If it is true that there are many thousands of Christian teachers working in the public schools of our land, why don't we hear more about them? If these adults have been so intimidated by their colleagues and the courts that *their* light is seldom seen, and their voice is seldom heard, can a Christian's child be expected to do better?

In the year 1212, sincere Christian parents of the medieval church decided to send their children to conquer Jerusalem and drive out the Moors. This Children's Crusade, as it was called, was a disaster. The children died in severe storms or were slaughtered by bandits and wild beasts. Those who survived were sold into slavery to the Moors and raised as Moslems. You cannot serve God by disobeying God.

A similar slaughter is taking place today. Some Christian parents send their children to the public schools to take them for Christ. Others are just sent to get an education. Some are sent just to get them out of the house. The result is the same. Casualties lie all around us. The few children who survive with their faith intact are more influenced than they are influential.

The growing numbers of parents who refuse to entrust their little lambs to the howling wolves *have* come to realize the obvious. They have come to realize that they are their children's keepers, protectors, and providers. They have come to realize that *God has entrusted the care, the nurture, and the education of those children primarily to them*. Not to the State. Not even to the Church. But to them. To the parents.

That's what God has ordained. So says Moses (Deuteronomy 6:4-9). So says Jesus (Luke 15:11-32). So says Paul (Ephesians 6:4).

And so says Solomon:

> Behold, children are a heritage from the Lord, the fruit of the womb is His reward. Like arrows in the hand of a warrior, so are the children of one's youth. Happy is the man who has his quiver full of them (Psalm 127:3-5).

Today's Christians talk at length about *stewardship*—the supervision or administration over goods that are not their own. Christians generally realize that those things are theirs to use, but they have no

absolute right over them. Sadly, this excellent emphasis on stewardship has been limited in most cases to three basic areas: time, talents, and possessions.

Although the Bible speaks authoritatively and precisely about
our responsibilities in those areas, it also defines stewardship much
more comprehensively. "The earth is the Lord's, and the fullness
thereof, the earth and all those who dwell in it" (Psalm 24:1).
Everything is the Lord's—including our children. We are stewards
over our children.

It's terribly unbiblical for Christians to think of conception and
childbirth simply as nature taking its course. Children are gifts from
God. He sovereignly gives to each couple as He wills. And He
never makes mistakes. The fruit of the womb is *God's* reward, created in *God's* image, and He has the absolute right over them. Parents
are only given stewardship of their children; to *keep* and care for
them, with their eyes fixed on God's standards.

God does expect Christian parents to raise children who will
have a godly impact in the world, who will give honor and glory to
Him all the days of their lives. That is why the Psalmist describes
children as weapons against the powers of darkness:

> Like arrows in the hands of a warrior are sons born in one's
> youth. Blessed is the man whose quiver is full of them (Psalm
> 127:4-5).

Parents think of all kinds of nicknames and cute words to call
their children. "Arrow," however, is one few of us would have used.

In Solomon's day, Israel had no factories for mass-producing
arrows, each identical to the others. Instead, each warrior hand-
crafted his own. A tree would be cut into boards, boards into strips,
and from those strips a warrior whittled his arrows.

Because arrows were handmade, no two of them were quite alike,
and few were perfectly straight. So when the warrior would pull one of
those arrows out of his quiver to use in battle, he would have to
remember the peculiar bend and other characteristics of that arrow.
Then he'd aim it and pull the string back according to those unique
traits. Aimed correctly, the arrow would hit the mark; if not, the arrow
would miss, possibly costing him his life, and his army the battle.

What Psalm 127 is telling us, as moms and dads, then, is that we need to have a "warrior mentality." We need to be shaping our kids into arrows that will fly straight to the target God has set for them. If we're not carefully shaping and aiming our arrows, others will try to steal them and shape them for *their* use. What's worse, they will aim our children at targets of their own choosing. We should never be surprised if we are wounded by the members of our own family, if we have allowed sworn enemies of Christ to aim them.

In thinking this way about our children and our responsibilities toward them, we need to take care not to underestimate the potential of any child. It's so easy, for example, to look at a child with a special disability and think, "How can this child ever make a difference in the battle?" Time after time, these children have shown that they can.

After a workshop I conducted in Ohio, a mother came and told me she had a child with Down's Syndrome. She explained that several people in her area felt that such children simply weren't being challenged enough; they weren't being expected to aspire to their greatest potential. Perhaps they could do more if someone expected more. These people also believed, she said, that since typical programs for Down's Syndrome children segregated them from other students, they effectively encouraged them to assume the behaviors and attitudes of the most helpless among them.

With that perspective, these people decided to follow an alternative program for Down's Syndrome children, one that dealt with them individually, encouraged them, and challenged them to their utmost potential. The program worked. In fact, they have found that some of the children in their program have progressed to the point that their IQ scores are within the lower range of that of a normal child! Potential is in God's hands. Anyone can count the seeds in an apple. Our God can count the apples in a seed. Never underestimate what God may do through your child.

Imagine a group of Down's Syndrome kids someday standing up to the enemies of God in the education bureaucracy and to legislators: "You have plans for how to deal with us and others with disabilities, and we'd like to say a word about that. You think we don't have potential, that we can't contribute anything to society, that our lives aren't worthwhile. But you watch what we can do." Our God gives gifts of different kinds to all his children.

Who knows what God will do with *your* children if you train them up in the way they should go and aim them into the world as arrows in His service?

Thousands of years ago, God called on Abraham to start a godly dynasty, a family that, for generations to come, would stand for His righteousness in a sinful world. He wanted Abraham and his seed to be strategic weapons in His hands for the overcoming of evil. Today He is calling us to do the same thing—to start dynasties of right-eousness. He is calling us to establish our homes as embassies of His Kingdom and to train up families that will be powerful weapons in God's hands for years to come.

That, ultimately, is what is at stake in this battle. Will our chil-dren be an extension of our lives and our faith, or of others'? Whose side will they be on? Will we be wounded by the members of our own household? Or will our children have an impact for God's glory?

There is a battle raging, not *for* the public schools, but *with* the public schools, over who will aim our children. And if we are going to win this battle, we must take the initiative.

Summary

Our Christian children need more than public school prayer to a nameless, unknown god in a moment of silence.

Our Christian children need more than a New Age creationism without the Creator.

Our Christian children need *Christian* education.

Where shall they find it?

In Christian homes, of course, with Christian moms and dads.

To rephrase Professor Bloom, Christian education fully admits that it wants and needs to produce men and women who have the tastes, knowledge, and character supportive of, and constructive within, the Kingdom of God.

After all, it is His Kingdom that will last forever.

The advantage of a public education is that it enables you to despise the wealth which it prevents you from achieving.

Russell Green

T W O

MASS-PRODUCED
EDUCATION

The bell rang and the children drank their last few drops of milk as they scurried from the lunchroom to the classroom. John Franklin rose from his desk as stragglers slipped in, and he invited everyone to gather around his chair.

No invitation needed, really. This was the best part of the day. Sometimes Mr. Franklin told a tale, sometimes he just talked with the kids. So the class crowded at his feet. A popular fellow with his students, the young teacher drew one little girl into his lap just as she started to sit beside him.

"What do you think about God, Deborah?"

She paused. A difficult question for many third-graders. And Deborah was especially shy.

"I don't know."

"Aha," Mr. Franklin said, "so you're an agnostic." He spelled it for her. "You're not too sure about God. Well, do you know what? I'm an atheist because I *know* God doesn't exist." All the children were visibly impressed.

Down the hall on another day, a school counselor tested a little third-grade Christian girl for values clarification. The counselor posed the problem of which people should be thrown out of a heavily-laden life raft. The girl gave an answer that involved men making a voluntary sacrifice of life for the sake of women and children, rather than self-centered, cold-blooded murder. The counselor was irritated by her answer and responded, "Well, you're just answering that way because you're a Christian. There is no right answer."

Those two episodes, and dozens of others like them, finally led Theresa Martin to leave her teaching post at that suburban elementary school in Texas. "I taught for several years in the public school," she said. "I know what goes on there. That's the main reason we're home schooling our own children now. We don't want them to have to put up with that."

Unfortunately, the values of the teacher and counselor at her school aren't unusual. Psychology Professor Paul Vitz of New York University explains:

> Given the overwhelming secular philosophies characterizing American education in the last fifty years, it is to be expected that leaders in education will now differ markedly from the general American public in the area of basic moral values. This has been documented in the *Connecticut Mutual Life Report on American Values in the 80s*, where, for example, it is reported that 65 percent of the general public describe abortion as morally wrong while only 26 percent of education leaders describe it as wrong; 74 percent of our education leaders say that abortion is "not a moral issue." Likewise, on many other traditional values and moral issues, the education leaders are reported to be markedly more liberal than the public. Education leaders, for example, overwhelmingly say homosexuality and lesbianism are not morally wrong.[1]

Of course, this testimony hardly suggests that every public school teacher shares those values. Far from it. But those who don't are intimidated into silence. If they are fighting at all, they're fighting a lonely battle.

Professor Vitz goes on to say:

> Some teachers, of course, still introduce God, prayer, and traditional concepts of right and wrong into their teaching or school activities. But teachers and schools that permit them are rare and becoming more rare all the time, for such actions are probably illegal according to recent Supreme Court decisions. At any moment, complaints or lawsuits could come these teachers' way. *Such teachers and schools within public education are a dying breed, operating outside professional and legal support.*[2]

In Nashville, Tennessee, a high school girl asked her mother, who was already home schooling two younger siblings, to home school her, too. The reason? She was being socially ostracized by peers because she wouldn't go along with activities contrary to her morals. She had refused, for example, to keep lookout at the door to the girls' rest room while her friends used drugs inside.

In a wealthy suburb of Los Angeles, police raided the lockers of the local high school on a tip that drugs and weapons would be found there. Over sixty guns and a substantial amount of illegal substances were confiscated. That, in and of itself, was not surprising. But over 70 percent of the guns and drugs were found in the lockers of respected young ladies from "good homes." When interviewed by the police, the young women responded that no one could protect them from the gangs active in the high school. Not the principal, not the police, and surely not their own parents. The only way, they said, to have any safety on campus was to ally themselves with one gang or another and agree to hide drugs and weapons.

The situation with gangs is out of control. Thanks to our mass media and the movies, no town or village has been spared. Good kids, from otherwise strong families, are being intimidated into joining the gangs just in order to have protection. Parents and other adults look weak and foolish in their hand-wringing and empty lectures. Until authorities and parents have the will to take decisive action, the kids are right. They have to go along in order to get along.

The Making of Books

You can learn a lot from your child's textbooks if the schools will let you see them. Textbooks, of course, are the foundation of any school curriculum, the heart of what gets taught. The following is what Professor Vitz found in his study of the books commonly used in American public school classrooms:

These studies make it abundantly clear that public school textbooks commonly exclude the history, heritage, beliefs, and values of millions of Americans. Those who believe in the traditional family are not represented. Those who believe in free enterprise are not represented. Those whose politics are conservative are almost unrepresented. Above all, those who are committed to their religious tradition—at the very least as an important part of the historical record—are not represented.

Even those who uphold the classic or republican virtues of discipline, public duty, hard work, patriotism, and concern for others are scarcely represented. Indeed, the world of these virtues long advocated by believers, as well as deists and skeptics such as Thomas Paine, Benjamin Franklin, and Thomas Jefferson, is not found here. Even what one might call the "noble pagan" has ample reason to reject these inadequate and sentimentalized books which seem to be about an equal mixture of pap and propaganda.

Over and over, we have seen that liberal and secular bias is primarily accomplished by exclusion, by leaving out the opposing position. Such a bias is much harder to observe than a positive vilification or direct criticism, but it is the essence of censorship. It is effective not only because it is hard to observe—it isn't there—and therefore hard to counteract, but also because it makes only the liberal, secular positions familiar and plausible. As a result, the millions of Americans who hold conservative, traditional, and religious positions are made to appear irrelevant, strange, on the fringe, old-fashioned, reactionary. For these countless Americans, it is now surely clear that the textbooks used in the public schools threaten the continued existence of their positions.[3]

It is interesting to note the huge support that welled up in the mid 90s in response to conservative talk show hosts. After being relegated to the backwaters of the media for so many years, their traditional views received a ready audience, especially among the young. Unfortunately, what they offered was conservatism without Christ, which is capable of just as great evil as liberalism without Christ. The former can be very mean in its drive for efficiency, the latter tends to be very foolish economically. Only those who fear God are capable of rising above these abuses of power to bring wisdom and compassion together in good laws. In the meantime, our public schools continue to be bastions of the most liberal points of view and, hence, the most foolish budgets. And a great deal of those budgets go to the purchase of textbooks.

Textbooks, like teachers, can speak their message very softly. For example, one health book treats the unborn child in two very different ways. The chapter on fetal development shows cross sections of the womb holding a tiny child with eyes, ears, a mouth, arms, and legs. The chapter on birth control and abortion features cross section drawings of the womb, too. But, here, saline and D&C abortions are said to be performed on blue blobs. No child exists.

Manipulative, anti-Christian, politically correct teachers and textbooks aren't public education's only problems though. Public schools fail to make the grade in other areas as well. Not only are they morally impoverished, they are scholastically bankrupt.

Failing to Educate

When the National Commission on Excellence in Education gave a report to Congress, these were some of its findings:

International comparisons of student achievement, completed a decade ago, reveal that on nineteen academic tests, American students were never first or second, and, in comparison with other industrialized nations, were last seven times.

Some twenty-three million American adults are functionally illiterate by the simplest tests of everyday reading, writing, and comprehension.

About 13 percent of all seventeen-year-olds in the United States can be considered functionally illiterate. Functional illiteracy among minority youth can run as high as 40 percent.

The College Board's Scholastic Aptitude Tests (SAT) demonstrate a virtually unbroken decline from 1963 to 1980. Average verbal scores fell over fifty points and average mathematics scores dropped nearly forty points.[4]

In 1992, the system is still in crisis. In his book, *Illiterate America,* Jonathan Kozol paints the picture more graphically:

Twenty-five million adults cannot read the poison warnings on a can of pesticide, a letter from their child's teacher, or the front page of a daily paper. An additional thirty-five million read only at a level which is less than equal to the full survival needs of our society. Together, these sixty million people represent more than one-third of the entire population.

Given a paycheck and the stub that lists the usual deductions, 26 percent of adult Americans cannot determine if their paycheck is correct. Thirty-six percent, given a W-4 form, cannot enter the right number of exemptions in the proper places on the form. Forty-four percent, when given a series of "Help Wanted" ads, cannot match their qualifications to the job requirements. Twenty-two percent cannot address a letter well enough to guarantee that it will reach its destination. Twenty-four percent cannot add their own correct return address to the same envelope. Twenty percent cannot understand an "Equal Opportunity" announcement. . . . Over twenty percent cannot write a check that will be processed by their bank—or that will be processed in the right amount. Over forty percent are unable to determine the correct amount of change they should receive, given a cash register receipt and the denomination of the bill used for payment.

Thirty percent of naval recruits were recently termed "a danger to themselves and to costly naval equipment" because of an inability to read and understand instructions. The Navy reports that one recruit caused $250,000 in damage to delicate equipment "because he could not read the repair manual." How many more illiterates are now responsible for lower-level, but essential, safety checks that are required in the handling of missiles or the operation of a nuclear reactor?[5]

The failure of our educational system to do its most basic job begins at the lowest grade levels. William Bennett, United States Secretary of Education under the Reagan Administration, reported in 1986 that:

Ninety-one percent of thirteen-year-olds were unable to write an adequate persuasive letter; eighty-four percent of thirteen-year-olds (and virtually all nine-year-olds) were unable to write an adequate imaginative essay; eighty-one percent of eighteen-year-olds (and ninety-seven percent of nine-year-olds) couldn't produce a simple factual description requiring no opinion, creative thinking, or argumentation.[6]

Then he cited a recent study showing that, in math, the *highest*-scoring American fifth-grade classes failed to match even the *lowest*-scoring Japanese classes.[7] It has become a joke that although American students are scoring lowest in math, they score highest in self-esteem about their failure. In the face of these and other embarrassing results, Bennett joined fellow former Secretary of Education Lamar Alexander in calling for the dismantling of the Department of Education. Test scores simply don't support the continued funding of its programs.

We can begin to understand these scholastic failures when we look at the declining level of competence among the new generation of public school teachers. While there are still many good and even outstanding teachers to be found, there are also many others who fall far short of the mark. Consider these examples:

One of the contributing factors to the academic decline in public schools is the training and competency of teachers. For instance, according to a study released in July 1991 by the Carnegie Commission on Science, Technology, and Government, more than 80 percent of math instructors are deficient in math! Also the study found more than two thirds of elementary school science teachers lacking adequate preparation in science.[8]

Rita Kramer documents in her recently released book Ed School Follies: The Miseducation of America's Teachers, that most future teachers who are trained in the nation's teacher colleges primarily receive indoctrination in politics rather than learning.[9] She explains, "Almost nowhere did I find teachers of teachers whose emphasis was on the measurable learning of real knowledge."[10] She spent a year touring fifteen teachers' colleges from Columbia to UCLA. Kramer concludes that America's schools of education are appalling. She found that among teacher-educators today "the goal of schooling is not considered to be instruction, let alone intellectual, but political."

The students attending teachers' colleges and pursuing education degrees are, on the average, below average on SAT scores. Consistently, these students who are planning to major in education scored below the national average. Such students' average verbal score is 406 (out of a possible 800; national average is 422) and their math score average is 441 (out of a possible 800; national average is 474).[11]

Why is the competence level dropping in the teaching profession? One reason is that competent women and blacks of both genders have many more career options today. Before 1970, the teaching profession was the domain of the best and the brightest women and minority personnel. Today teaching school is becoming a dumping ground for those students who cannot make it in any other job market. Education courses are being viewed as the soft, easy track through college. As the old saying goes, "Those who can, do. Those who can't, teach." And, we might add, those who can't teach, now administrate.

Imagine the frustration of the dedicated and talented teachers in the public schools. They have to work around all the incompetent teachers because it is all but impossible to fire them. The teachers' unions protect their members, but not the students of their members. One teacher described the process of transferring a rotten teacher from one school to another as, "Pass the trash."

Regardless of the reasons behind it, the picture is clear. Many public school teachers are dangerously unqualified to teach.

Lack of Discipline

Not only do many public schools fail morally and scholastically, they also lack necessary discipline. A survey conducted by the National Education Association turned up these findings:

Some 110,000 teachers—one out of every twenty—were physically attacked by students on school property during the 1978-79 school year. Another 10,000 were attacked by students off school property. The 110,000 victims represent an increase of 57 percent over the estimated 70,000 teachers who were attacked during 1977-78. Of the teachers who were attacked, an estimated 11,500 required medical attention for physical injuries and an estimated 9,000 required medical attention for emotional trauma.[12]

A more recent study shows that the threat to teachers themselves continues: in the preceding twelve months, 640,000 teachers had had personal property either stolen or intentionally damaged by students, and approximately 80,000 teachers had been physically attacked by a student.[13] It's no wonder that a survey taken by the Metropolitan Life Insurance Company found that 95 percent of all teachers believe a much higher priority should be given to school discipline and safety! It's also no wonder that a 1986 Louis Harris poll revealed that 55 percent of classroom teachers have seriously considered switching to a different career (low pay also being an important factor).[14]

Attorney Chris Klicka has compiled extensive documentation of the moral crisis in the public schools. In his book *The Right Choice; Home Schooling* he reports the findings of The National Educational Goals Panel, released in 1991. The panel announced that nearly one out of five public school teachers reported being verbally abused by students in the previous month. Eight percent reported being physically threatened, while two percent reported being physically attacked during the previous year.

Students also abuse other students, both directly and by damaging the school facilities. It's estimated that every month some 282,800 people, most of them students, are physically attacked in schools. In addition, $600 million is spent each year to repair vandalism.[15]

Perhaps even more galling than the lack of discipline, however, is the utter impotence of local school authorities to do anything about it. Because of legal and administrative constraints, little if anything can be done to remedy the situation. For example, writer and school critic Joseph Adelson tells of a situation in his hometown in which older children were bullying and extorting money from younger children on the way to and from junior high school. Complaints to the principal were ineffective, so a PTA meeting was called.

In a heated discussion, the parents were given a summary of the legal restrictions preventing any kind of corrective or disciplinary action by school officials, including the principal. The basic message was that nothing could be done. Says Adelson, the parents were "incredulous, then angry and disgusted."[16] And well they should have been. But in a lawsuit-happy society, school authorities are afraid to discipline students. They are caught in the trap of their own liberal views on child training.

Another major problem facing kids in public schools today is the epidemic of drug abuse. In 1986, California Attorney General John Van De Kamp said, "It is a sad and sobering reality that trying drugs is no longer the exception among high school students. It is the norm."[17] The United States Department of Education agrees: "The United States has the highest rate of teenage drug use of any industrialized nation. The drug problem in this country is ten times greater than in Japan, for example. 61 percent of high school seniors have used drugs."[18]

The problem isn't just that kids are *using* drugs at school; that's also where they're *getting* them in the first place. A study of teenagers who called a cocaine hot line showed that 57 percent of them buy most of their drugs at school.[19]

Damaging Moral Values

While children in public schools today are not being taught Biblical values, they are being taught values. Valueless education is impossible. So if the values being taught aren't Biblical, what kind are they? One mother and former teacher from Oregon summarized for the Department of Education what she had observed while sitting in on a workshop for students aged fourteen and up. She quoted the instructor as saying, "Your parents' values are different from yours. They grew up at a different time and have a different field of experience."

Her description of the class went on, "She—the instructor—told them that they are beginning to take risks, that is, make decisions that their parents might not approve, that they are running into conflicts with their parents, and that up to now, their parents have gotten away with directing or controlling them. Every mention of parents was negative."

This same mother later attended another workshop at which instructors "told those receptive teenagers that there are *no* objective standards of morality, and that truth is relative and can mean anything they want it to mean." The mother continued, "When I interjected that truth does not change, and that morals do not change, that it is attitudes toward morals that change, he [the teacher] replied, 'Yeah, on one level I think I hear what you are saying, but I have a real difficult time with that, because my truths change from day to day.'"[20] This is what is called "values clarification," and it is a standard part of almost every public school curriculum in America.

Another popular public school subject with clearly immoral overtones is sex education, which is growing ever more popular in light of the apparent teenage pregnancy epidemic and the terrifying increase in AIDS and other sexually transmitted diseases. While the subject of sexual intercourse could be taught responsibly in the context of Marriage Education, the kind of instruction reported by this father is all too typical in the public schools of the eighties:

> In my son's fifth-grade health class, all questions were answered without regard to a moral right or wrong. Homosexuality was presented as an alternative lifestyle. Sexual activity among fifth graders was not discouraged, since it was feared that the students might be embarrassed and not ask additional questions.

> I was present when a plastic model of female genitalia with a tampon insert was passed around to the boys so they might understand how tampons fit. Birth control pills were also passed around and explained. Anal intercourse was described. At no time was there any mention of abstinence as a desirable alternative for fifth graders. The morality that was taught in the classroom that day was complete promiscuity.[21]

The idea of sex as a privilege reserved for married couples only is completely missing from the modern discussion. Words like adultery and fornication have been censored, due to their clear moral connotations. Is it any wonder that our social problems related to sexuality multiply?

One health and sex education textbook has this to say:

> Adolescent petting is an important opportunity to learn about sexual response and to gratify sexual and emotional desires without a more serious commitment. In many societies, premarital intercourse is expected and serves a useful role in the selection of a spouse. In such societies, there are seldom negative psychological consequences.[22]

Another student health text shows the following caption under a picture of two young men embracing: "Research shows that homosexuals can lead lives that are as *full* and *healthy* as those of heterosexuals."[23]

Not only is the content of these courses and the nature of teacher input questionable, but many teachers are not averse to instructing kids in this fashion without parental consent. Surveys show that most American parents oppose the teaching of sex education to their children without their consent, which is entirely understandable and well within the realm of traditional parental rights. Teachers, however, favor teaching it without parental consent by 61 percent to 36 percent.[24] In other words, there is a betrayal of trust here. These teachers no longer see themselves as working for the parents of the students, but as working for some liberal segment of the community against the wishes of individual parents.

Clearly, there is something terribly wrong in a school system that makes parents pay for a school that works against them.

Antipatriotic Teaching

Patriotism has virtually become extinct in America's public schools. Once again, this can be seen clearly in the textbooks commonly used. As part of his overall study, Professor Vitz looked at 670 stories and articles in third and sixth-grade reading books. This is what he found:

There are only five stories in all these books with any patriotic theme. Three of the five instances describe the story of the ride of Sybil Ludington in 1777.... This story is in many respects a feminist piece, and it has little of a specifically patriotic character.... To summarize: of the twenty-two textbooks, seventeen (over 75 percent) do not have one patriotic story. Furthermore, none of the patriotic stories has anything to do with American history since 1780—nothing for the last two-hundred years. Four of the five stories feature girls and are certainly at least as feminist in orientation as they are patriotic. Only one book out of twenty-two—one story out of 670—has a story with a patriotic theme that features a boy. These books do not have one story featuring Nathan Hale, Patrick Henry, Daniel Boone, or Paul Revere's ride.[25]

That kind of report would be hard to believe if it weren't from such a credible source. And it isn't just reading books; history books, too, often ignore key figures from America's past while featuring people of far less significance. For example, one fifth-grade textbook devotes seven pages to Marilyn Monroe while mentioning George Washington only eight times, and that without ever describing his accomplishments.[26] An eighth-grade text ignores American historical giants such as Ethan Allen, John Paul Jones, and George Washington Carver, but includes singers Janis Joplin, Bob Dylan, and Joan Baez.[27]

History books, in other words, have been reduced from halls of fame to galleries of popular culture or counter culture.

The antipatriotic bias isn't found just in textbooks, however. A Pittsburgh mother reported, "Plays presented to students with actors dancing on the United States flag are not uncommon and were a big problem here in Pittsburgh. Kids are definitely being programmed to accept a new global perspective.[28]

It's no accident that today's classrooms reflect this inaccurate, antipatriotic perspective. John Dewey, the father of modern American education, was himself a socialist, and he and his disciples, who have controlled American education since World War II, have subtly and actively promoted socialism's values at all grade levels.

They reasoned that an excessive nationalism and ethnocentrism was behind most wars. Therefore, they concluded, if people were taught that all the world is one, and that no culture or government or way of life was better than any other—if there were an uncritical openness to others in foreign lands—there would be no more reason for wars.

That naive intellectual perspective has been foisted upon American students in the years since—there is no one right way of thinking or believing or acting. There is no such thing as a fixed set of moral values. Everything is relative. "As long as what you want to believe works for you, makes you happy, and doesn't `hurt' anybody, that's fine with me"—so the notion goes.

The type of mind-set this has produced finds able exposition in Bloom's *The Closing of the American Mind*:

> There is one thing a professor can be absolutely certain of: almost every student entering the university believes, or says he believes, that truth is relative. If this belief is put to the test, one can count on the students' reaction: they will be uncomprehending. That anyone should regard the proposition as not self-evident astonishes them, as though he were calling into question two plus two equals four....They have all been equipped with this framework early on, and it is the modern replacement for the inalienable natural rights that used to be the traditional American grounds for a free society....The danger they have been taught to fear from absolutism [i.e., the belief that truth is *not* relative] is not error but intolerance. Relativism is necessary to openness; and this is the virtue, the only virtue, which all primary education for more than fifty years has dedicated itself to inculcating. Openness—and the relativism that makes it the only plausible stance in the face of various claims to truth and various ways of life and kinds of human beings—is the great insight of our times. *The true believer is the real danger.* The study of history and of culture teaches that all the world was mad in the past; men always thought they were right, and that led to wars, persecutions, slavery, xenophobia, racism, and chauvinism. *The point is not*

to correct the mistakes and really be right; rather it is not to think you are right at all. The students, of course, cannot defend their opinion. It is something with which they have been indoctrinated.[29]

In other words, categories of right and wrong are purely mythical, save one: the only wrong is to think you're right, especially about God and His Law. The only thing you can be sure about is that you can't be sure! There are absolutely no absolutes left.

The High Cost of Public Education
It would be bad enough if the bad education being given to America's children were a bargain-basement operation. Then we might at least have the small comfort of saying, "Well, I guess you get what you pay for." But the fact is that public education in this country is extremely expensive. Clearly, we're not getting our money's worth—not in academic quality nor in the values that are being instilled along with the ABCs.

In 1991-92, public schooling cost the American taxpayer $248 billion.[30] State-supported education is a huge enterprise, with 2.3 million classroom teachers and the largest union in the world. The federal budget for education is the second largest of all the government's expense categories; only the state welfare programs cost us more.

Where do all those dollars go? A great deal of the money subsidizes a phenomenally huge educational bureaucracy. In 1931-32, there were approximately 259,000 school districts across the nation, which were run primarily by locally elected school boards sensitive to local concerns.

By 1980, however, even though the student population had grown by millions, there were only about sixteen thousand separate school districts.[31] That means that there is only one district for every sixteen there used to be. Meanwhile, the administrative staff of those districts has grown more than a hundred-fold. And that doesn't take into account the thousands of bureaucrats running dozens of federal programs and the large bureaucracies at the state and consolidated district levels dictating policy to the local school administrators.

All those American tax dollars paying for programs, policies, and personnel that are destructive to the values of most of our citizens—there's something inherently unjust about that. Professor Vitz explains the injustice well:

> Let us recall what the central issue is: tens of millions of Americans are paying school taxes—each taxpayer is providing hundreds or even thousands of dollars a year—to support a system that fails to represent their beliefs, values, history, and heritage. Indeed, the present public schools are actively supporting anti-religious positions and pushing liberal permissive values and politics. This is a serious injustice. Quite simply, it is a classic case of "taxation without representation." We are being taxed to support schools that are systematically liquidating our most cherished beliefs. Thomas Jefferson—hardly a reliable friend of religion—stated the principle clearly when he wrote: "To compel a man to furnish funds for the propagation of ideas he disbelieves and abhors is sinful and tyrannical."[32]

Regardless of how unfair it is, that's the reality of American schooling today.

A Short History of American Education

Though modern historians may deny or ignore it, though groups such as the American Civil Liberties Union, the National Education Association, or the People for the American Way may abhor it, the fact is that many of the people who planted the seeds of this nation, starting with the Pilgrims, were Christians. Even those who came largely for commercial reasons, such as the Virginia Company settlers who founded the first permanent settlement at Jamestown, had, as a significant part of their charters from the King, a commission to spread the Gospel of Jesus Christ among the Indians. Not surprisingly, then, for hundreds of years education in this country was openly Christian. Solidly, unwaveringly Christian. A child's Bible was his reading text, and its God and Gospel stood at the center of all his lessons. In most communities, the local clergyman, likely the most educated person around, served as the parents' supplementary teacher, and he naturally (with the parents' blessings) sought to instill Christian character as well as knowledge.

Furthermore, their colleges, such as Harvard and Yale, (now, sadly, bastions of anti-Christian humanism), began as schools to train young men for the ministry. How far we have come!

In 1837, the first public school was started. The Massachusetts State Senate, under the leadership of its Unitarian president, Horace Mann, enacted the first state-wide system in which schools were centralized, state-controlled, and financed by property taxes. There was more politics than education in this reform. Until then, schooling had been the job of parents, clergy, and, in supposedly rare instances, private tutors. Mann's "Common Schools" were created to make benefits of education available to all children, not just to "the privileged, the educated, and the rich." Close examination of the evidence shows that the poor were being included in private education, and only those who did not want to go to school were missing out. There was no need for a public school except as a tool to undermine the church's influence in education. Some see this as a violation of the establishment clause because state funds were used to change the religious view of citizens.

Despite Mann's attempts to radically secularize the learning process, the Bible remained a primary text for those early state' schools. As constitutional lawyer John Whitehead writes,

> In looking at the historical record, one sees that religion was integrated into the public school curriculum. Textbooks referred to God without embarrassment, and public schools considered one of their major tasks to be the development of character through the teaching of religion. For example, the *New England Primer* opened with certain religious admonitions followed by the Lord's Prayer, the Apostles' Creed, the Ten Commandments, and the names of the books of the Bible.[33]

This is not surprising when you consider the quality of the private schools the public schools were trying to supplant.

Even so, the erosion had already begun. We need to be careful not to overlook the vast differences between the role of the *New England Primer* among the Puritans and "the teaching of religion" in mid-nineteenth century public schools. As Secretary of Education, Mann insisted on keeping the Bible in education, but his motives were skewed. As one historian writes:

> Mann was not interested in the Bible as a means toward promoting *Godliness* but rather *social efficiency*. Religion should be used because it is productive of civic virtue; social orientation was everything. Mann's basic principle was the pragmatic use of religion. The basic reference in religion is, therefore, not to God but to society.[34]

We would be amiss, then, to entertain romantic notions of yesteryear's public schools, imagining that a return to the past century would cure all our ills. Christian influences remained, to be sure, but the schools, once they became state-controlled, tax-financed institutions, out of the jurisdiction of parents, never provided the sort of moral and educational excellence necessary to train true disciples. Mann, and those who succeeded him, found a use in their public schools for "Thou shalt not steal" and "Thou shalt not bear false witness against thy neighbor," but they had little use for "God so loved the world that He gave His only-begotten Son," or "For by Him all things were created that are in heaven and that are on earth, visible and invisible, whether thrones or dominions or principalities or powers. All things were created through Him and for Him. And He is before all things, and in Him all things consist." Civil authorities seek only a useful deity, not a Lord.

A truly Christian education, on the other hand, necessarily needs all these things. As Martin Luther said of the schools,

> I am much afraid that the schools will prove the gates of hell, unless they diligently labor in explaining the Holy Scriptures and engraving them in the hearts of youth. I advise no one to place his child where the Scriptures do not reign paramount. Every institution in which men are not unceasingly occupied with the Word of God must be corrupt.[35]

As if in fulfillment of Luther's warning, in 1899, John Dewey began to inject his openly anti-Christian philosophy into American schools, divorcing the Bible from academics. While he taught at the

University of Chicago, Dewey published his strategy for using the public schools to create a socialist utopia. Later he became director of teacher training at Columbia University and set himself to changing the course of American education. The people he trained became the deans and professors at other education centers where they molded the next generation's teachers. We have been reaping the harvest of their sowing ever since.

The Humanist Manifesto, written in part by Dewey and signed by thirty-three others in 1933, presents the doctrines of secular humanism. Simply put, Dewey and his co-signers rejected God and deified "the good of humanity." All good works would be done, not for the glory of God, but for the good of mankind. But in elevating mankind to the level of God, in effect, the humanists devalued individuals to the level of human resources for use by the State. Personal dignity found in our creation in the image of God was traded for greater freedom from God's moral demands.

In 1963, Martin Luther's predictions came true. In a Supreme Court ruling, Bible reading in public schools was declared unconstitutional. God's Word was officially banned from public education. A short time later, the Court made it illegal even to post the Ten Commandments, the basis of all law, in a public school. And to this day, there is an ongoing legal struggle to secure the right of public school students to use school facilities for voluntary religious discussion during non-instructional periods.

The point is, though, the infamous 1963 decision, and those afterwards, marked no sudden change of course in American public education. The movement toward fully secularized education began formally with Horace Mann's first "Common School" in 1837.

Resistance to Reform
In light of all this bad news about the state of public education in America today, our first reaction might be that we should try to reform the system. That's far easier said than done, however. As Professor Vitz has stated:

> This suggestion makes those who know the public school system roll their eyes in disbelief—and despair. Over the years, many

waves of reform have washed over the schools with very little to show for any of them. The net result has been that the schools are either unchanged or worse.[36]

Why does real reform seem so hopeless? There are at least four major reasons.

First, the educational bureaucracy is a monolith. "The schools no longer respond to parents or taxpayers," Vitz explains. "They respond to their own bureaucrats, that is, to the federal and state systems that more or less control and support the schools. Such a huge bureaucratized system, primarily concerned with complex and changing laws and regulations, has almost no real capacity for any kind of internal, positive change."[37]

Second, local educators have lost their authority. "In recent years," Vitz says, "local educators not only have lost power and authority to federal and state bureaucracies, they also have lost much of it to political and legal forces altogether outside the schools."[38] For example, the courts have become actively involved in dictating school policies concerning school discipline, as well as in dictating curriculum. An incestuous relationship seems to exist between Federal agencies that develop curriculum and curriculum publishers who bid for the right to publish it, knowing it will be automatically approved. Goals 2000 and Outcome-Based Education are only the most recent examples of this top-down control of a "grass roots" movement in public education.

Third, the anti-Christian mind of the education establishment bucks reform. They see our concerns as sour grapes over our defeat. We've already seen how those leaders are at odds with the values of most Americans. As Vitz summarizes:

> For years the philosophy of education dominating the country's schools of education has been uniformly liberal, secular, and even anti-religious....Whether one calls it secular humanism, enlightened universalism, skeptical modernism, or just plain permissive liberalism, the bottom line is that a very particular and narrow sectarian philosophy has taken control of American education.[39]

Recently, Outcome-Based Education threatens to push public education even further toward the left fringe politically. As Cathy Duffy has documented in her book, *Government Nannies*, the education establishment has used public outrage to push its agenda farther and faster.

Finally, the National Education Association (NEA) stands as a major roadblock to reform. With 1.5 million members, it is the nation's largest union. And, as Vitz says:

> The NEA is not only large but it is also extremely powerful and politically active....There can be little doubt that the NEA has a secular and liberal political philosophy and that it has increasingly come to control education. Indeed, the biased content of [today's] textbooks...is congruent with the politics of the NEA, and the simplest description of these textbooks is that they are a slightly watered-down version of the NEA's own political and ideological stance.[40]

Vitz concludes, "Very simply, the enormous power of the NEA makes it inconceivable that public school reform either could occur or could remedy the textbook bias."[41]

In the light of these obstacles, we are left with a campaign of damage control. Our children cannot be set on hold until we fix the schools. They need a Christian alternative now. Even if we could change the course of the public schools, it would not spare the current generation the devastation of a public school education. As parents, we must support the efforts of Christian teachers in the public schools and pray for their success in reforming the system, but we must do so without putting our own children in harm's way.

Conclusion

Clearly, today's public schools have not only failed to instill and nurture Christian values, they have become actively hostile to those values. In their zeal to change society, they have failed to uphold even a semblance of academic excellence. They have betrayed the trust of parents. And, as if to add insult to injury, they are exorbitantly expensive. There is little hope that any of these situations will improve in time to benefit our children. We must seek out alternatives.

Fortunately, there are still two good alternatives available to Christian parents and their children. One of the most popular of those alternatives over the past thirty years has been the private Christian day school.

Is that the answer we've been looking for? Or is there something better?

Every education teaches a philosophy; if not by dogma, then by suggestion, by implication, by atmosphere. Every part of that education has a connection with every other part. If it does not all combine to convey some general view of life, it is not an education at all.

G. K. Chesterton

THREE

A CHANGE OF SCENERY

Karen spoke very little at supper. Though high school freshmen are wont to have their ups and downs, she typically gave her family an enthusiastic play-by-play account of the day, an up-to-the-minute update on the local news, and a status report on who was "going" with whom. But, on this night, she spoke only when spoken to.

Something had happened at her public school earlier that day that had left her really uncomfortable. She wanted to discuss it with her parents just to get it off her chest, but she really feared their reactions. When Karen's mother finally cracked the tension, she couldn't help answering honestly.

"Do you mind if I ask if something's wrong?"

Karen was so relieved that her mother had initiated the discussion. She began to pour out the story, telling her parents all about her health class. At her school, freshmen were required to take the class in the spring.

For the past two weeks, the class had learned about the reproductive system, and the lectures had moved from a discussion of puberty in general to a series of lessons on the anatomy of the sexes. Today's lesson, especially lively, had centered around birth control: the pill, the diaphragm, spermicidal jelly, vaginal cream. The teacher cited the advantages and drawbacks of each. None of these, he pointed out, protects a couple from AIDS. Only the condoms give any degree of protection. And then the teacher produced a couple dozen condom packets and passed them out to the class.

"Everybody was laughing, especially all the guys," Karen said. "I thought he was giving them to the guys so they'd have them `just in case.' But he told the girls to go ahead and open the little packets. Then he had the guys stick up their index fingers and we had to put the condoms on them."

41

Her parents were stunned, outraged. And the next day, they let the principal know it. Karen finished that year at her high school, but her parents immediately began to seek a schooling option. They found it in a local Christian school.

Karen started classes there the next fall and made the most out of the new experience—finding more friends, enjoying a Bible class right after math, praying before school. But, during the previous summer, her parents had read a host of books about Christian education—what it was, and what it wasn't—and had come to expect a lot.

Now they were disappointed.

Not totally, of course. Though they were happily assured that the Christian teachers in Karen's new school would never distribute condoms to their classes, they couldn't see that the basic *substance* of Karen's education differed appreciably from what she had received at the public school. The Christian school seemed to be a cleaned-up version of the public school.

Over the past thirty years, Christian schools have been springing up all across the nation. Today there are roughly 18,000 of them, and new schools are constantly starting at a rate of one every ten hours. More than one and a half million children are now enrolled in these schools.

The Christian school movement was by far the fastest growing segment of American education, public or private, until home schooling. It continues to be the most popular response to the anti-Christian teaching and plummeting educational standards found elsewhere. The desire to see children raised in a Christian environment and with Christian character is the primary concern that drives Christian school growth.

The typical Christian school is preferable to the typical public school. In the Christian school, the various subjects are generally taught from a traditional perspective, and most teachers are themselves believers who try to set good examples before their students. But Christian schools, as with any institutions, are not without their problems.

Chinks in the Christian School Armor

Christian schools fall short of the Biblical ideal in at least five areas. Now, understand, these five problem areas are necessarily generalizations, and of course there are always exceptions to any general rule. A given school may do a better job in one or more of these areas than most others. When it comes to evaluating specific schools, each must be considered individually, and on its own merits.

But a solid case can be made for the following assertions:

First, the sad fact is that many Christian schools are simply a cleaned-up version of the public school approach. They remove most of the objectionable moral content; they may hold chapel services; their students may memorize Bible verses; and they present God as the Creator of the universe. But the distinction too often stops there. If the teaching staff is recruited from the state teachers' colleges, which is too often the case, the difference between a Christian school classroom and a public school classroom can be very small.

The fact is, inserting a Bible class into an otherwise secular curriculum does not a *Christian* school make. Jay Adams writes, "Often such a course is cosmetic, the 'proof' that a school is 'Christian'. It duplicates material taught in Sunday school and church. *Everything* that is taught in a Christian school should be taught Biblically, from a Biblical perspective, not just the Bible class."[1]

The Christian school should be more than a good non-public school. It should do more than merely "baptize" secular structures "unconverted."

This failure of the typical Christian school to provide a complete education from a Biblical perspective has a parallel in Jewish history. In order for the people of Israel to worship Him properly, God ordained first, the tabernacle in the wilderness and later, the Temple in Jerusalem. Acceptable worship meant, among other things, worshiping in the right place and in the right way—the place and way God had prescribed.

When Babylon conquered Israel and took her people captive to other lands, it became impossible for them to return to Jerusalem in order to worship God in the proper way. Further, conquering armies destroyed the Temple. There was no Temple to worship in.

In response to these crises, the system of local Jewish synagogues developed. For many years, the Jews had no other place to worship. The synagogue was their only alternative, and it became the new traditional place of worship.

During the reign of Persian King Cyrus, however, work to rebuild the Temple began under the direction of Zerubbabel and Joshua. Once it was completely restored, it should have become the focus of Jewish worship again, consistent with God's instructions. For the most part, there was no longer any need for local synagogues. The Jews, however, continued to worship in synagogues, ignoring God's Law. They borrowed methods of worship from the land of their captivity. The restoration was incomplete. But God honored the synagogue system anyway when Christ Himself taught in them.

In a similar way, Christian schools, by essentially imitating the public schools, using state certification, teaching in a manner inconsistent with the Biblical mandate to the family, have also strayed from God's design. We've been "exiled in the land of captivity" for so long that even when we "come back into the land," we continue in patterns learned from those who do not know or honor God's Word. The Christian school restoration is incomplete. We have borrowed too freely from the land of captivity. But in spite of this imperfection, God blesses the Christian schools with His presence.

Second, the Christian school violates the principle of the power of companionship because it is normally structured in an age-segregated way. The importance of who children spend their time with, adults versus other children, can't be overstated. "Those who walk with the wise will be wise, but a companion of fools will suffer harm" (Prov. 13:20).

The Bible gives us an excellent illustration of this principle in the story of three generations in the same family. First there is Solomon, famous for the great wisdom with which God blessed him, making him the wisest man who ever lived (apart from Christ, of course). The story of Solomon's asking God for wisdom shortly after he became king of Israel is told in 1 Kings, chapter 3. But what was the background from which Solomon made that request?

Solomon wrote in Proverbs 4:

When I was my father's son, tender and the only one in the sight of my mother, he also taught me, and said to me: "Let your heart retain my words; keep my commands, and live. Get wisdom! Get understanding! Do not forget, nor turn away from the words of my mouth....Wisdom is the principal thing; therefore get wisdom....Exalt her, and she will promote you; she will bring you honor, when you embrace her" (verses 3-5, 7-9).

Solomon's father, David, clearly had a tremendous influence on him. He taught him to go for wisdom. When the offer came from God, Solomon asked for wisdom. That wisdom shaped Solomon into Israel's most successful king and the world's richest man until he turned his back on God late in life. But his great accomplishments were the result of a godly father's influence.

Solomon himself raised only three children. His only son was Rehoboam, who came to Israel's throne when Solomon died. Unfortunately, as Rehoboam was growing up, his father violated his own counsel by failing to walk closely with him and to teach him. In 1 Kings, chapter 12, we are told that Rehoboam grew up with a group of other boys who influenced him negatively.

When Rehoboam deliberated his first major decision as king, he first consulted the elders of Israel who had been advisers to Solomon. He rejected their counsel, however, and turned to the young men with whom he had grown up. Their advice contradicted the elders', but Rehoboam followed it anyway, rending the kingdom into two factions that would war against each other for generations.

I'll speak about peer dependency in the next chapter, but the stories of David, Solomon and Rehoboam make the potential danger clear. Age segregation undermines wisdom and maturity. And the problem can be just as severe in Christian schools as it is in the public schools.

Third, there's an understandable but nonetheless harmful double-mindedness in the mission of most Christian schools. On the one hand, they want to offer Christian parents and children a good moral environment. A big reason for their popularity is the desire of parents to remove their kids from the immoral influences and lack of discipline in the public schools. "Bad companions corrupt good character."

On the other hand, many Christian schools also want to have an evangelistic outreach into their communities. They want to win the lost to Christ. But bringing in problem children with uncooperative parents introduces the very immoral influences the Christian child's parents are paying to avoid. Proverbs counsels us to "remove the scorner from your midst and strife will cease." In fact, Christian schools often attract some of the worst behavioral cases, students who have essentially been thrown out of public schools for criminal activity. All too often, Christian schools unintentionally end up acting as "reform schools" which cannot remove the scorners. Granted, there is a real need for Christian educators to open and run Christian reform schools. But such schools should not operate under the same roof with a school for children entrusted to them by Christian parents. This double-mindedness weakens the schools' ability to achieve either objective. It should be an <u>earned privilege</u> to attend a Christian school.

Fourth, there's a strong tendency in Christian schools for parents to abdicate their God-given responsibility for the education of their children and to pass it on to the schools. Parents who send their children to Christian schools are concerned about what's happening in the public schools and recognize that they would be acting irresponsibly by leaving them there. Once they put them into the Christian programs, however, they unconsciously assume that all is now well—the Christian administrators and teachers can be trusted to train their children properly. They breathe a sigh of relief as they tell themselves they have one less thing to worry about.

Such an attitude, though understandable, is dangerous. The Bible makes it clear that the primary responsibility for the education and training of children rests with the parents. Regardless of how it is pursued, education is always more effective when parents actively participate in the process.

Finally, Christian schools that utilize the classroom inevitably face the same practical problem as the public schools—the division of the teacher's time and attention between many different needs and students. With twenty or twenty-five students in a class, a teacher is forced to aim each lesson at the average child, thus failing to suit the lesson to a number of students at both ends of the spectrum. There's no way that twenty-five different children can be at the same level of understanding and ability. The brightest child will be bored, while the slower student will be frustrated. This is a result, not of inept teachers, but of classroom size and structure.

These five criticisms are certainly not intended to represent a frontal attack on Christian-school teachers and administrators. Indeed, many of them acknowledge these problems and have been frustrated when their own dreams of real Christian education have confronted these obstacles by experience in the reality of a Christian school. Jay Adams writes,

> All over America I have talked with Christian school teachers and administrators who feel cheated. They tell me that they entered the field of Christian education with great expectations that have not been realized. They had hoped to be involved in something dramatically different from the education that the world doles out, but in this they have become disappointed and disillusioned. Better than anyone else, they know that, basically, with very few exceptions, what they are doing is not all that different from what their counterparts down the street are doing day by day. They are thankful for Christian fellowship, freedom to talk about Christ, to pray, to use the Scriptures and many other such things, which do create a far more wholesome atmosphere, but they yearn for *more*, something more that will enable them to do what they thought they were going to do—give their classes a truly wall-to-wall, ceiling-to-floor Christian education.[2]

Again, the problems of Christian schools discussed here are generalizations, and each school deserves an evaluation on its own merits. Generally speaking, despite their problems, they represent a much, much better choice than today's public schools. In the next chapter, however, we'll consider why home schooling is the best alternative of all. And in a later chapter, we'll discuss how Christian schools and home schools are working together for the benefit of both.

Summary

Out of public school horrors, droves of Christian parents have rushed their children into private Christian schools. The phenomenal growth of such schools over the past three decades is very encouraging. And while they are certainly a better place to have our children than in public schools, they, too, have their problems.

First, many Christian schools only clean up the public schools' practices. Objectionable material is ferreted out; Bible verses are memorized; and God is mentioned without fear of a lawsuit. But these can be shallow, cosmetic tokens of what a thorough Christian education should be.

Second, age-segregated peer pressure is part of the Christian school experience. The school structure is not Biblical.

Third, many Christian schools reveal double-mindedness. They want to give Christian children a godly moral environment while they enroll troubled non-Christian students in the interest of evangelism. The two ministry missions fight against each other and betray the trust of Christian parents.

Fourth, too many Christian parents put their children in a private Christian school and then abdicate their responsibilities as the primary educators. This is clearly not Biblical.

Fifth, Christian schools that use classroom organization inevitably face the problem of dividing the teacher's time among a class full of students, all of whom have differing needs.

It is not enough to study our subjects in the light of Scripture; we must allow God's light to illuminate the very methods of our teaching. We must not only build on God's Word, but also build in submission to God's Word.

A genuinely Biblical education demands more than just a change of scenery. It demands a comprehensive reformation. We must design a system and approach to education that honors all of God's Word.

I learnt Greek letters as I learnt English letters at home. I was told about them merely for fun; while much else I learnt during the period of what is called school education; that is, the period during which I was instructed by somebody I did not know, about something I did not want to know.

G. K. Chesterton

THERE'S A BETTER WAY

"What is home schooling really like?" you may be wondering. "What kinds of things do you do all day long?"

Well, let me give you an idea of a typical day of home schooling in my family. After the children get up, dress, brush their teeth and comb their hair, we gather as a family for breakfast. One of us may share what he/she studied in quiet time with God's Word. Then, as in most homes across America, it's time for school. Instead of heading off down the street, however, we just go to different parts of the house.

I have the privilege of teaching Alex and Bret (age 5) and Sarah (age 4) their phonics. We sit in an easy chair (the same one Sono used when she nursed them); and after a quick review of the last lesson, we start the next. While I am working with one, the other two are working on their *Ready Writer* pages, a preschool handwriting program.

Joel, now age eleven, hits his Saxon Math while he listens to music. Our strategy is to start with least favorite subjects so the children have the energy and attention needed to tackle them. They are motivated to keep studying because they are always working *toward* the subjects and activities they enjoy most (their delights). Between each of the subjects, they may take a short break to do a household chore from their *Choreganizer* chart; and then it's back to their studies. They normally get the bulk of their studies done before lunch.

Every day each one uses one of his breaks to complete a major chore, such as vacuuming carpets or cleaning the kitchen. Now, that may not sound like much of a break to you, but it's a definite change from sitting and studying. It gives them the mental rest they need while simultaneously teaching them to be a responsible member of the family. Work, like study, is part of life.

After studying through the morning, we normally break for lunch around noon. Afternoons are set aside for "delight-directed" activities; Joel can take as long as he wants with his favorite subjects, just as long as he completes his other assignments. Alex and Brett love art, for example, and if we were to let them start with that in the morning, they would be drawing all day! So, art has to wait until the afternoons. Joel has piano lessons on Tuesday mornings.

Because he's doing things he enjoys, Joel works all through the afternoon. We plan to have supper around five or six o'clock, and we try to follow that with a time of family Bible reading, though I have to admit, like most busy families, we're not as consistent about that as we'd like to be. We also have family nights—we have a family over for dessert. Twice a month we go to the home-school skating party—350 and growing.

Home Schooling—What It Is and Is Not

As you can see from this brief description, home schooling is neither a radical departure from classroom instruction nor a carbon copy of what happens in a typical school. All the basic subjects are covered in an intensely personal, closely supervised and intentional way, but in a non-institutional setting.

Some of the most prominent names in our culture's history were either educated at home or were privately tutored: George and Martha Washington, James Madison, John Quincy Adams, Benjamin Franklin, Patrick Henry, Abraham Lincoln, Winston Churchill, Woodrow Wilson, Theodore Roosevelt, Franklin Roosevelt, Hans Christian Anderson, Pearl Buck, Charles Dickens, Mark Twain, Noel Coward, John Stuart Mill, Leo Tolstoy, George Bernard Shaw, C. S. Lewis, Wolfgang Amadeus Mozart, Andrew Carnegie, Pierre DuPont, Cyrus McCormick, Douglas MacArthur, George Patton, Alexander Graham Bell, Pierre Curie, Thomas Edison, Albert Einstein, George Washington Carver and Albert Schweitzer. That is a very impressive track record. But, remember, in the day in which these people were home schooled, home schooling was like home cooking. No one made a big deal about it. You just taught your children what you knew, at home.

Many parents today are afraid they would not be able to uphold a high standard of educational excellence. They are afraid they would not be able to do an adequate job. Study after study and case after case, however, consistently demonstrates that home schooling does a much better job of educating than do the conventional schools. For example, a Stanford University study found that home-schooled kids scored significantly higher in achievement, behavior and social perception than did public-schooled kids. A study by the National Home Education Research Institute in 1990 showed that home-schooled children scored an average of thirty percentile points higher than the national average on standardized tests. A 1995 study of Canadian home schoolers confirmed this result within a distinct culture. Home school works.

Again and again, these results are borne out in the experience of home-schooling families all across North America. A high school graduate in Wallace, Nebraska, , began home schooling her daughter who had been failing sixth grade. The mother taught her daughter for only an hour or two a day; they spent the rest of each day working together in the family hotel. In nine months, the daughter's academic standing had risen almost three grade levels. This is not an isolated case. As I write this, I have over ninety thousand alumni of my Home Schooling Workshops, and these kinds of results are common.

In Booneville, California, three boys have been taught at home on their family's sheep and goat ranch. The parents were worried a few years ago that, because of their limited knowledge about the natural and physical sciences, their oldest boy might have trouble grasping those subjects. At eighteen, however, he received scholarship offers from both Harvard and Yale. He graduated with honors in biology from Harvard. His brother went on to attend Harvard as well. So much for their parents' fears!

Although better academics isn't the only reason, or even the main reason, parents decide to home school, it is a good reason. The education is of high quality.

The Abandoned Basket of Benefits

Imagine a family walking down a dusty country road, the mom and dad carrying a picnic basket between them. It's a heavy, well-packed basket, full of delicious foods they prepared at home. As the family strolls along, not even thinking there might be an alternative to what they're doing, they meet someone on the road.

"Why are you carrying that basket?"

"It has all kinds of good things in it for our family," the father answers.

"Oh, but you don't need that," the person says. "There's a different fast-food place very few blocks all the way up this road. Any time you get hungry, you can just stop in at one of those places and pick up a hamburger, chicken, french fries, or whatever your heart desires. The food is good and it doesn't cost much. In fact, it probably costs much less than what you put into your basket. You don't need to waste your energy lugging that heavy picnic basket around."

That sounds good to the family, so the parents decide to put the basket down and go on without it. They continue down the road, and soon they come to the first fast-food restaurant. When they turn in, they discover that, sure enough, the food is good and not very expensive. They set off down the road again, and when they get hungry, they turn into another fast-food place. This time they find that the food isn't quite as good, and while it's still not expensive, it costs a little more than the food at the first place.

Continuing down the road, the family obviously gets farther and farther away from its picnic basket. Finally, they reach what they think is a point of no return. Despite the fact that they are entirely dissatisfied, despite the fact that with each fast-food restaurant they enter, the food gets worse, the prices, higher, they continue to trudge along.

More than we'd like to admit, that is the story of the American family. We've been convinced over the years that others outside the family can do a better job of providing things that the family had always provided for itself in the past. Institutions that specialize in everything from fast-food to fast times, from public schools to public health, have wooed us with a promise that they can meet our needs at lower prices and with better quality. What we've found, though, is that the farther we get away from the family unit, the higher the prices go and the poorer the quality gets.

Sadly, even though most families are frustrated with this state of affairs, we've somehow convinced ourselves that we just cannot go back. The Waltons may make a good television show, but we'll never see a front porch like that again. I'm convinced, however, that if we remember the best things from our heritage and take them with us as we step into the future, we can restore what's best for our families. We haven't reached a point of no return. Not yet.

The Educational Advantages of Home Schooling

Home schooling offers many advantages over classroom instruction, no matter where that classroom is found. Let's look at just a few of them.

The significance of parents: "Daddy, you're the best daddy I ever had!" my four-year-old daughter gushes.

I just say "Thank you", not willing to make the observation that I am also the only daddy she has ever had. But there's a tremendous educational benefit simply because of that fact. When Mom and Dad are doing the teaching, the "best" people in the child's world are involved. By accepting the modern idea that the school classroom is the only proper place for education, we've given up a tremendous advantage.

You as a parent have higher credibility in teaching your own child simply because you are the parent. The most significant people in a young child's life are usually his mom and dad. That's why you are the "best".

Now remember that "significance" is a subjective thing, a matter of personal preference and judgment. Each child's own parents are the best to each child. This is not an objective truth. For example, the mathematical statement "two plus two equals four" is an objective reality. There's no personal taste involved, and it's not open to dispute (at least not among rational people). On the other hand, if I say I think chocolate ice cream is the best flavor of ice cream made, I'm talking about a matter of personal preference. You might think differently and choose to assert that vanilla is the best flavor of ice cream going. I really can't argue with you on that score because it's an entirely subjective issue. We are both right, even though we disagree.

In the same way, you may actually be something less than the world's best parent. You might also think that you can't possibly educate your child as well as a college-trained, state-certified teacher might. But because, subjectively, you are the most significant and important person in the world to your child, you have greater credibility with him. You can get more mileage out of instructional time than anyone else could. And that is an objective reality. That's one reason why the mom in Nebraska could teach her daughter so effectively, even though the girl studied only a couple of hours a day. It is your child you can teach effectively, because you are the greatest person he has ever known.

Children naturally love and admire their parents and want to imitate them. The bonding that takes place in the early days of a child's life, the love and care that parents give a child, these are the things that lead a child to place so much importance on his parents. It is an awesome responsibility and a wonderful opportunity—to teach.

This is one of the ways God has designed us as human beings: making young children very teachable and wanting to be like the most significant people in their lives. And those "most significant people" are meant to be the parents.

If we give our children over to the other schools, surrendering our responsibility to train and shape them, it won't be long before "teacher worship" begins to develop in the children. The children will come to respect and admire their teachers more than any other persons, and begin to emulate them. Then one day little Johnny will come home from school, and we'll try to tell him about the Pilgrims getting off the boat at Plymouth Rock, thanking God for their safe arrival, and he'll put his little hands on his little hips and say, "That's not the way the story goes! The Pilgrims stole the Indians' land. You don't know; you're not the teacher."

"Teachers don't make mistakes, Mommy; teachers correct mistakes," Johnny will tell us. "And if you disagree with my teacher, you must be wrong." If we disagree, we undermine the teacher's ability to teach. Who is to be trusted most by the child?

Moral purity. Earlier we looked at the kinds of immoral, anti-Christian values that are being taught in public schools today. As a parent, you're left out in the cold. You have no say in the values that are transferred to your children. By teaching your child at home, however, you can control the values that are instilled. You can choose a curriculum that undergirds your faith and presents it attractively and persuasively.

In the area of sexual conduct and self-control, for example, a recent survey of teenagers found that they think everyone *expects* them to become involved in premarital sex. Many of them said no one had ever given them any positive reason *not* to get involved. But as your child's teacher, *you* can help your child develop the values, moral convictions, and strength of character to remain pure for marriage. In today's world, moral purity has become a matter of life and death. Today's sexually transmitted diseases are totally unforgiving.

Individual instruction. A third big advantage of home schooling is the higher level of individual attention each student receives. In a classroom of twenty or more students, a teacher must split her time and attention into very small segments. She can't give much individual instruction or encouragement. And the students who demand the most attention are not always those with the greatest needs. They may be those who simply make the most noise.

Individual attention, however, provides a much better foundation for teaching and learning. It's no coincidence that wealthy people have often chosen to hire private tutors for their children. In a one-on-one relationship, the teacher can get to know the student and his needs much better, discover the best ways to motivate the child, and best slant the pacing and content of study to the student's interests and abilities.

A teacher with only a few students can monitor the level of difficulty of what is being taught. If the child finds the material too easy, he'll soon become bored. If he finds the material too difficult, he'll soon become frustrated. Either extreme hinders effective education, whereas almost any subject can be learned if the right level of difficulty is presented and maintained.

In the typical classroom, however, the teacher is not able to closely monitor the level of difficulty for each student. He cannot shape the curriculum so that each student is properly challenged. Instead, he has to aim for the average child, with the inevitable result that a number of students on either side of average will suffer.

When a child is given the right degree of difficulty in his studies so that he enjoys the challenge and experiences a feeling of accomplishment, he will improve in those subjects and carry those positive feelings into other areas of life. A bored and frustrated child, on the other hand, will feel like a failure; that feeling, too, will be carried into other areas of life, causing him to be afraid to try new things or learn new subjects.

Children will have good days and bad days, just like the rest of us. On a good day, a teacher may be able to ask more than usual of a student, and the child will handle it with ease. On a bad day, the opposite is true. In a typical classroom, however, the teacher can't gauge which students are having good and bad days and then adjust the day's lessons accordingly. But the home-schooling parent can.

Feeling of security. Our children need to be able to abandon themselves to study. For that, they need to feel secure. When a child feels insecure, he will hold back and play it safe. He won't try new skills for fear of ridicule by others.

Children are normally more secure at home than anywhere else. When a child is sick, or hurt, or afraid, where does he want to go? Straight home, usually into Mom's arms. All too often, though, we unknowingly send our sons and daughters off to environments rife with disruption and insecurity.

When our son, Joshua, was five years old, my wife and I thought that since he was an only child, he needed more social interaction. So we sent him to preschool three days a week at a nice Christian school. It was just half a day each time. Over a six-week period, however, we watched our son's personality change dramatically, and we didn't know why.

At home, he'd suddenly burst into tears for no apparent reason. I have to admit that, for a while, we tried to discipline him for his "outbursts" because we didn't think there was any reason for it. We were wrong. He had a reason; the stress caused by his insecurity at school was overloading his emotional circuitry. His attitude toward schooling could have been permanently damaged at that point.

We found out what was going on by talking to the teacher and speaking at length with Joshua. Poor little Joshua, wanting to please his mom and dad so much, had bottled up all his fears and anxiety about the school. It turned out that some of the children in that school lacked discipline, and he didn't know how to cope with their methods of handling conflict. After being pushed down and intimidated a few times, he began to hide inside himself. Our cheerful little guy was caving in to fear. He didn't understand what was happening, and he didn't know what to do.

Fortunately, I was studying education at the University of Dayton at the time. From my reading there, I began to realize that the classroom compromises the needs of children in favor of school administration. A classroom cannot meet the needs of a child like Joshua. It simply cannot provide the kind of secure environment children need. As long as a child is afraid, he is not free to explore and try new things. He is not free to learn.

Healthy socialization. Building on Joshua's story, a fifth big advantage of home schooling is, ironically, in an area where the criticisms have been most strident—namely, socialization. Home schooling provides a much healthier and better socialization process for children than the typical classroom.

Common sense tells us, and innumerable studies verify, that people become like those with whom they spend large amounts of time. The writer of Psalm 1 was well aware of this principle thousands of years ago. "Blessed is the man who walks not in the counsel of the ungodly, nor stands in the path of sinners, nor sits in the seat of the scornful." Similarly, we read in Proverbs 13:20, "He who walks with wise men will be wise, but the companion of fools will suffer harm." Paul also reminds us that "bad company corrupts good character."

When children spend ample time with their parents and siblings in a warm and loving atmosphere, they usually learn to enjoy being with all age groups, including their own. By watching and imitating others, they learn politeness, and they learn to express themselves confidently with good conversational skills.

On the other hand, when children spend more time with their age-mates than they do with their parents (as is the case with typical classroom schooling), they tend to become oriented towards their peers. This is because children need a sense of identity. They need to know who they are in relation to other people. This helps them feel secure. And if they're spending more time with other children their own age than they are with parents, they will be powerfully motivated to establish a new identity in relationship to those peers. They will feel pressured to please their foolish age-mates.

When a child is put into an age-segregated setting (school), no one knows his mom and dad, his brothers and sisters, his neighbors or his church acquaintances. So he's forced to start from scratch in developing an identity in this new environment. He does this by reaching out to a few other kids who look and act enough like him so that he feels there's some rapport. A peer group is born.

These peer groups create a strong sense of identity for the young people in them. And to help foster that sense of identity, they'll often develop distinct "uniforms"—dress, vocabulary, habits, and gestures. The kids know who's in which group, and that becomes the basis of their identity away from home.

The sense of identity these groups provide can be so strong that, at some point, when the values of his group conflict with those of his family, the child will be forced to make a choice between the two. He may not openly rebel, even if he decides to follow the group, but he'll quietly find ways around his parents' authority. He becomes deceitful. Many a parent is shocked to discover his child is in a gang or using drugs. It all flows from the power of companionship.

Some parents fear that a child who isn't exposed to the "real world" while he is young won't be able to cope with it later. But don't worry, the real world has a way of intruding into everyone's life. And if you look around, you will see that the "real world" comes to church. You don't have to go to a school to find the harsh side of life. In our media-intensive society, you cannot hide for long.

Nobody is better off by being exposed to evil, in whatever form, and that's especially true of children who are struggling through their formative years. What they need in order to cope with the "real world" is not a detailed knowledge of evil, but an experience of the value of strong and godly character. The home is much better suited to providing that experience than any school.

The best approach to socialization is to simply be a household open to hospitality. Rather than allowing your child's friends to remain locked into an age-segregated relationship, welcome them as friends of the family. As one mom put it, "The best way to improve your child's friends is to adopt them." Be a wise companion to the youngsters in your church and neighborhood, so that they can become wise.

Flexibility. Another strong advantage of home schooling is the flexibility it allows in the educational process. In school, teaching is strictly confined to the classroom setting and the prescribed hours of attendance. In the home, however, there are constant learning opportunities. Little Johnny helps Mom sort and wash laundry. He helps Dad change the oil in the car. Flexibility not only affects schedule and opportunity, but motivation as well.

Suppose, for instance, a child is motivated to work harder by the prospect of completing formal lessons in half the usual time. The home school can accommodate him. He can enjoy the rewards of his diligence there. But, in the classroom, this is just not possible. If he finishes early, he will just have to wait for others to finish. On the other hand, if a child is having trouble with a particular subject at home, he can work at it longer. In the classroom, where schedules are rigid and the needs of the other students have to be accommodated, he is forced to hurry up. If a child has a strong interest in science, the family that home schools can creatively direct and motivate the child in that area. They can plan extra field trips to museums, nature hikes, experiments and projects. They can, in short, be flexible and responsive. The program can be tailored to the student's needs and interests. This is only possible in a tutoring environment like that of a home school.

Parental significance, moral purity, individual instruction, high security, healthy age-integrated socialization and flexibility—these are just a few of the benefits of home schooling. Home schooling offers these and other advantages over the typical classroom. Home schooling would be worth pursuing even if there weren't a Biblical mandate to train our children along these lines. But there *is* such a mandate, a clear call from God to be responsible for the full development of our children. We'll explore that mandate in the next chapter.

Summary

There *is* a better way. And home schooling is it.

Home schooling represents no radical departure from the structure of traditional education, nor is it something that merely suits the fancy of fanatics. Home schoolers can boast a long history of success—their children achieve more and behave better.

When you decide to home school, know that you enter it with the advantages stacked on your side.

You are your child's parents, and you know him best. You are his most "significant other." This is your first advantage. Use it to his best advantage.

Because you're able to shape your child's moral environment, you're also able to shape his moral character.

Home schooling allows individualized instruction. You can monitor your child's progress and make adjustments accordingly, so that he is neither bored nor frustrated.

Your child needs to feel secure in order to study well. A school classroom can't give him as much security as the four friendly walls of your own home.

Where will your child experience the healthiest socialization: in the age-segregated classroom as the companion of his age-mates, or at home in the instruction and discipline of the Lord? Face it. Children imitate the people they spend the most time with. "Blessed is the man who walks not in the counsel of the ungodly" (Psalm 1), but "the companion of fools will suffer harm." (Proverbs 13:20). Time with well-mannered people normally translates into well-mannered children. On the other hand, more time with peers may mean your child becomes peer-dependent and loses his identity. Your child should spend more time with adults and children of all ages.

Finally, under what conditions will your child most likely be able to pursue those things that delight him: in the daily grind of the typical school, or in the flexible structure of the home school? Your home school allows you and your child to capitalize on constant learning opportunities around the home and to strike out on your own—visiting museums, taking hikes, doing special projects together.

Clearly, there *is* a better way.

A school should not be a preparation for life. A school should be life.

Elbert Hubbard

THE BIBLICAL BASIS
OF EDUCATION

The Apostle Paul said, in Romans, that when sinful men and women rejected God and refused to give Him the glory He is due, they "became futile in their thoughts, and their foolish hearts were darkened" (Romans 1:21). No matter how much sinful people learn, they're never able to make sense of their knowledge; they can never understand how one thing they know relates to the other things they know. They lack insight and wisdom. This is why the most intelligent—and often even the most sincere—people in the world frequently have a very unclear picture of what life is all about. It is even possible to be an intellectual fool.

Take, for example, the very intelligent and pious Pharisees. Jesus described them as "blind leaders of the blind" (Matthew 15:14). They had a distorted perception of God and, therefore, knew nothing about living a godly life. But their self-deception in no way limited their confidence in what they taught. They were sincerely wrong.

If your physical vision is unclear and you find yourself stumbling around in the dark, the obvious solution is to cast more light on your path. In a similar way, we need a clear light in order to bring the spiritual and intellectual world into focus. In fact, the Bible is the only "light" that can put what we know into proper perspective.

Now, admittedly, in the area of science, for instance, the Bible doesn't provide all the technological specifics we need to run the machinery of modern culture. We won't find in its pages the detailed plans for how to build a computer or how to develop wheat that's resistant to insects and disease. That's not what the Bible is for. But, at the same time, we can't properly understand those scientific minutiae or why they are useful and meaningful, unless we look at them in the light of Holy Scripture with believing eyes. We have to learn about the God who, long ago, made the universe out of nothing and even now holds it together by His power, in order to use technology and science properly.

In a similar way, the Bible isn't intended to be a textbook for teachers and school administrators. It doesn't pound out every detail of proper pedagogy. But it does tell us everything we need to know to evaluate education—to tell the basic difference between good education and bad. Without it, educational excellence is utterly impossible. We would be blind leaders of the blind, walking in the darkness of our own opinions.

Let's turn on our Biblical lamps, then, and see what we can learn about educating our children.

The Biblical Teaching Staff

The first thing that becomes clear when we look at education in the light of God's Word is that it is *parents* who are called by God to train their children.

Moses tells us in Deuteronomy 6:6-7, "These words, which I command thee this day, shall be in thine heart; and thou shalt teach them diligently unto thy children, and shalt talk to them when thou sittest in thine house, and when thou walkest by the way, and when thou liest down, and when thou risest up." The "words" Moses is talking about here are the statutes of the Lord. Godly parents, he says, are to teach their children what God requires. They are to teach their children God's principles at all times, in all places, in all ways. Earlier, in Deuteronomy 4:9, Moses said, "Only take heed to thyself, and keep thy soul diligently, lest thou forget the things which thine eyes have seen, and lest they depart from thy heart all the days of thy life; but teach them to thy sons, and thy sons' sons." Here Moses was instructing the people of God to remember the powerful things they had seen the Lord do on their behalf and in judgment on sinful nations (Deuteronomy 4:3-4).

It is important that we remember the things we've seen God do and the answers to prayer He's provided. We must not discount our own experiences just because they haven't been made into a movie or written up in a newspaper. The experiences God brings our way are valuable, especially in times of difficulty when we're tempted to doubt God's care and power. And we need to pass our experience on to our children.

But, of all the things the people were to remember, there was one that Moses, under the Lord's leading, considered most important: "Specially the day that thou stoodest before the Lord thy God in Horeb, when the Lord said unto me, 'Gather me the people together, and I will make them hear My words, that they may learn to fear Me all the days that they shall live upon the earth, and that they may teach their children'" (Deuteronomy 4:10).

We must never forget that God is holy and righteous. He is the Judge of sin. There is a proper sense in which we ought to fear Him, especially if we're living with unrepented sin. That's why the book of Proverbs tells us several times that the fear of the Lord is the beginning of wisdom; those who fear God as they should, say "no" to sin. This truth is something we should teach our children, as a foundation for all other study.

In the New Testament, the Apostle Paul reminds us of this same calling. In Ephesians 6:4, we read, "And you, fathers, do not provoke your children to wrath, but bring them up in the training and admonition of the Lord." In adding "of the Lord," Paul distinguishes the discipline and instruction he has in mind from that received from the readers' own parents, or even from that recommended by "the child training experts" of the day. Paul knows that God Himself is the everlasting Father. He is the original "Good Dad." That means that God deals with those who love Him as children. Wherever we find God disciplining or instructing His children, we find principles of good child training. He is to be our example in how we train up our children, not our own parents and not the experts. If we draw near to God through Jesus Christ, and behold Him in spiritual worship, we will become more like Him. And we will take on His style of parenting as well.

In all of my work with home schoolers and other parents, this principle is held up as a basic guideline. We want to identify God's attitudes, God's methods, and God's principles of child training.

One such principle is found in Proverbs 22:6: "Train up a child in the way he should go, and when he is old he will not depart from it."

The words *train up* are not framed as a mere suggestion. They are a command. But Solomon's choice of words also tells us something about how to carry out that command. In the original Hebrew, *train up* means "to touch the palate." In Solomon's day, Hebrew mothers would feed their children by first chewing their own food very carefully and, then, touching a little of it to their child's palate. With that intimate sharing, the mother would instill in her child a taste for the very same foods she enjoyed. She was giving him a taste for whatever delighted her own palate. To translate the metaphor educationally: parents are to instill in their children a taste for their own delights by enjoying things together with their children. By working together, studying together, playing together, and simply living the Christian life together, our children develop, not just a tolerance for what is right, but a deep inner yearning, an appetite for the things that have touched their palates as children. These tastes will form the basis for their lifetime of joyful obedience to the Lord.

The phrase "in the way he should go" makes it plain that the kind of *training* Solomon has in mind is training in righteousness. Though each child is expected to be unique and the specific methods of training will have to be tailored to his individual bent, the target is basically the same. The archer has to aim each of his arrows according to its unique characteristics, but the target is still wisdom and righteousness.

These and many other verses of Scripture reveal a few fundamental principles that are worthy of being noted. First, these instructions are not requests or suggestions—they are commandments. The instruction and discipline of our children is something God *requires* of parents. To willfully disregard these commandments is sin. "Children, obey your parents in the Lord, for this is right," Paul wrote in Ephesians 6:1. That's a pretty short list of people to obey. It's not that children can disobey every other authority in this world. No, they must obey these other authorities because their *parents* require them to. Ultimately, in a child's life there is but one authority, that of his parents in the Lord.

Second, the training we're to do is not simply academic, although it certainly includes sound scholarship. We are also commanded to prepare each child to walk as a faithful Christian in all areas of life. An arrow has two ends. On one end is the arrowhead. We want sharp arrows, academically speaking. But on the other end of the arrow, we find a delicate guidance system; fletching made of feathers, to be exact. We want our arrows to travel toward their target without deviation. This corresponds to the development of moral character. A proper education will work on both ends of the arrow (i.e., both ends of the child) at the same time. Although scholarship is obviously important, a sharp arrow is worthless without proper direction. And a blunt arrow, even if it hits its target, will have very little effect.

Is home schooling for everyone? This is a touchy question. Single-parent families come to mind. Health crises and other extenuating circumstances intrude, suggesting that home schooling cannot possibly be for every family. But what about home cooking? Would we excuse parents from feeding their children under these or any other difficult circumstances? Of course not. Children have to eat. Where there is a will, there is a way to feed your kids.

Well, children also have to be instructed. Every child's mind has an appetite for knowledge. But rather than fan the fires of controversy, let me rephrase that first question. Rather than ask, "Is home schooling for everyone?" let me ask, "Should every Christian home be a place where children are instructed?"

If the answer is yes, then welcome to the home school movement. Take your place as the God-ordained faculty of God's educational program for children. It remains for us only to define what an education is for and how much of a child's education should be provided at home.

The Purpose of Education

What is education? What most modern philosophers and educators fail to realize is that we really can't answer that question until we first know what *man* is, for it is man that we educate.

The modern secular form of education is based on the ancient Greek conception of mankind as *homo sapiens*, or "thinking man."

Sadly, that view represents an incomplete and inadequate perspective. It suggests that the most basic difference between man and other creatures is his intellect, his ability to reason. But being "made in the image of God" implies something even more basic than intellect.

According to the Bible, man is not merely another species among many. He is not a naked ape. He is not simply *homo sapien*. Man is a moral being. Man can worship. He is, instead, *homo adorans*, which means "worshiping man." "The chief end of man," says the Westminster Catechism, "is to glorify God and to enjoy Him forever." And what a privilege that is! No other part of creation has the opportunity to worship and commune with the heavenly Father voluntarily, intelligently, and intimately. This is what sets man apart from the rest of creation. It is the moral dimension of man's design.

When we acknowledge the majesty of God and His lordship over our lives, coming to Him through the atoning work of Jesus the Son, we are born again into a right relationship with Him, the relationship lost when Adam sinned. Because of our new birth, we're able to worship Him in spirit and in truth, to offer up what the psalmist called "a sweet-smelling sacrifice" of praise. And that, in turn, makes fellowship with Him possible. This fellowship is the greatest joy because it is the purpose for which God made us. It is also the basis of all morality. It is the opposite of sin. Many people are basically unhappy with their lives. The reason is that their sin has put them out of fellowship with God. They're attempting to live contrary to the purpose for which God gave them life—a sure formula for frustration.

It only stands to reason, then, that one of the primary purposes of education is to prepare people to be born again and then to worship and fellowship with God. Certainly we want our children to fulfill the calling for which they were made. We know that that's the only way they can ever have true joy in this world and in the next. And it is the foundation on which all other obedience must be built. The arrow has need of moral character to guide it through the adventure of life. No amount of intelligence can give moral guidance.

In addition, the Bible makes it clear that *homo adoran* does not worship God best in isolation. He is a social being by design. Thus, education is to benefit our society and the Church by equipping us to fulfill our part and take our place in the community of faith. The Ten Commandments, which are the basis of all law and moral codes, instruct us first, to worship God, then, to love and respect the lives, rights and property of others.

For human beings to live together in peace and harmony, we need to love God and keep His commands. We do this by walking in the Spirit of Christ, loving one another in practical and ever more skillful ways. Education instills these things in the young. But in teaching them to the young, those who are older are stretched and renewed in their own commitment to God. Parents learn more by trying to teach their children than children learn by being taught. The one who prepares the lesson learns most. That is as God intended it to be. One reason children are given to us is to help us grow up.

A complete Christian education will also equip each student to fill his station in God's design for society. It will include both vocational and avocational training. The ability to establish a business and manage a godly home will be high on the list of priorities. Such a household will then become an embassy of God's Kingdom in the community, a source of strength from one generation to another.

And finally, we are created for rulership in time and eternity. The adventure of the Christian life is infused with practical challenges which require a useful knowledge of God's creation, understanding of God's principles of government, economics, history, science and human culture. "Great are the works of the Lord. They are studied by all who delight in them" (Psalm 111:3). All areas of study are delightful to those who can see how each area relates to all the others in God's plan.

A complete education will not overlook or despise these "humanities", or the "Liberal Arts", which are in fact the "arts of freedom". Don't allow a fear of liberal ideas to rob you or your children of your heritage. These studies are necessary to prepare each generation for participation in the act of governing—a responsibility that comes with living under a representative government and having the right to vote. In a democratic republic such as ours, these "ruling class arts" are not just for the wealthy and the powerful.

They are for everyone. The fact that our major liberal arts colleges and universities have become politically liberal is a call to attack, not retreat. One small candle can dispel a lot of darkness.

The Church itself is better off when the home is the center of this kind of education, for then it enjoys a steady flow of competent and Biblically-qualified church leadership. It's interesting that the qualifications for church elders include a heavy emphasis on family management. Paul wrote to Timothy, "An overseer then must be above reproach, the husband of one wife, temperate, sober-minded, given to hospitality, able to teach...one who rules his own house well, having his children in submission with all dignity (for if a man does not know how to rule his own house, how will he take care of the Church of God?)" (1 Timothy 3:2,4,5).

We've all seen those who keep their children under control, but with no dignity at all—those who have to scream at their children. That is not God's best. A man who has to scream at his children will also have to scream at the church, if he is ever placed in leadership there. Paul said that a man who would be a leader in the church has to have first trained his own children properly. That's the surest proof that he'll be able to lead the church effectively. Conversely, a man who doesn't control his family with dignity, who hasn't succeeded in training his own children in Christian living, is a living illustration of his inability to lead in the household of faith. We cannot cross a chasm of immaturity on a bridge of merely academic training. Growing up takes time.

In other words, the skills that a parent develops in training his children are directly transferable to leading the church, and even the society at large. Good fathers are fit for leadership because their households provide models for the rest of the community to follow. You can point them out to onlookers and say, "Watch those families, and follow their example. Make your households into what theirs have already become." People learn best by seeing a flesh-and-blood example, and families that work as a household to fulfill their own ministry provide living illustrations to others. Thus, good home-centered training not only shapes children into effective arrows for society, but it also transforms parents into strong future leaders for the church and community.

The Biblical Means

When it comes to the means of education, there are a few general, but crucial, principles we need to consider at this point. The first is the primacy of the Bible in our instruction: "All Scripture is given by inspiration of God, and is profitable for doctrine, for reproof, for correction, for instruction in righteousness, that the man of God may be complete, thoroughly equipped for every good work" (2 Timothy 3:16-17).

The last part of that verse summarizes beautifully what education is all about: that the man or woman of God may be "complete," "mature," "thoroughly equipped for every good work." But such completeness is possible only when the Bible is given its proper place as the light by which all things are evaluated. Without the Bible, we are walking in the dark on every path of life.

The Apostle Paul was writing to his disciple and fellow-minister, Timothy, whose heart was so in tune with Paul's own that the apostle addressed him as "my true son in the faith" (1 Timothy 1:2). Immediately preceding this passage, Paul provides the educational context, saying:

> But as for you, continue in the things which you have learned and been assured of, knowing from whom you have learned them, and that from childhood you have known the Holy Scriptures, which are able to make you wise for salvation through faith which is in Christ Jesus (2 Timothy 3:14-15).

Apparently, Timothy had been "home schooled" in the Scriptures from a very early age by his mother and grandmother, and it had been done effectively so that he had grown to be a mature and useful servant of God. Isn't this what we want for our own children?

But the question arises, how do we teach the Bible to children in the home? We can read to them, of course, beginning with the Bible stories. We can have family devotions. We can make certain they're in church and Sunday school each week. But, in Deuteronomy, chapter 6, a more comprehensive program is outlined: "Thou shalt teach God's laws diligently unto thy children, and shalt talk of them when thou sittest in thine house, and when thou walkest by the way, and when thou liest down, and when thou risest up."

Education is supposed to go on virtually all the time—morning, noon, and night. It doesn't come just in occasional periods of formal teaching, but continually, as a lifestyle. How can that be? Surely we're not supposed to be teaching the Bible every waking minute, are we? Well, frankly, yes. But that is not as drastic and formidable as we might think if we approach it in God's way.

First, there should be times of "diligent" and even "formal" train-ing, such as I've described above. Regular, planned times of instruction like these should be a part of the daily lifestyle of every Christian fami-ly. No family is going to do this perfectly day in and day out, but, like meals, it is the cumulative effect that counts. What's important is that a steady diet of spiritual feeding is being provided for our children. The church services and Sunday school should be used to give direction and to set the pace for the Bible instruction going on at home. No need to operate two distinct programs of study. Study as a family at home whatever your pastor is preaching.

Second, as a means of backing up our formal times of study and instruction, we should take advantage of the informal opportunities that come our way almost every day. Children are naturally curious, and we should encourage them to ask questions. Even without their questions, they'll often say or do things that can be turned to educa-tional use.

Each of us has opportunities to teach our children. We simply have to learn to see them for what they are and take advantage of them when they come along. Now, I admit, this isn't easy. It takes alertness, often when we're tired and would rather just administer discipline or ignore the question. But if we're going to take seriously our responsibility for the training of our children, then, with God's help, we mustn't let those golden opportunities slip away. They comprise a very important side of home schooling.

Third, whether we realize it or not, we're actually teaching all the time. In fact, the most powerful teaching is done when we're not intentionally teaching at all, but merely living through our daily routine. The most effective teaching is communicated by our exam-ple. Our children are constantly watching us, and they pick up our values, our mannerisms and our priorities, little by little, day by day. Thus, the way they'll learn the most about how the Christian life is lived is not by what we say when we're trying to teach, but by the way we actually live when we think school is out.

Stop and think for a minute about your own parents. As you've gotten older, haven't you recognized more and more that you do and say a lot of things just like they do? You probably eat like one of them, walk like one of them, and use a lot of the same words and expressions. They influenced you in ways they may never have intended, or may even regret.

But let's apply this principle to the positive characteristics we want to instill in our children. If we want our kids to love to read, the best thing we can do is to enjoy reading ourselves. If we tell our kids they should read for pleasure while we spend all our time parked in front of a television set, what message do you think they're picking up?

Likewise in spiritual matters: if we want our children to delight in Bible study, they should see us reading and studying and applying the Bible. That's the only way they'll ever believe it's important to us and something worthy of their time and effort. If we want them to learn to seek God's guidance and help in prayer, they should see us doing the same. They should catch us making our requests known to God and overhear us thanking Him even before He answers. If we want them to worship God, they should see that we consider it important enough to be in church on Sunday and to enjoy the praise and worship.

Jesus summarized this principle: "A disciple is not above his teacher, but everyone who is perfectly trained will be like his teacher" (Luke 6:40). The student who admires his teacher doesn't just acquire the same knowledge, Jesus was saying. The two will eventually think alike; they will talk alike, even live alike. Our teacher should be the Lord Jesus Himself, and we, in turn, should teach our children. We should be able to say to them, as Paul said to the Corinthians, "Imitate me, just as I also imitate Christ" (1 Corinthians 11:1).

As parents, we have received this charge and this challenge from God, regardless of whether we choose to school our children at home or send them to a classroom. Whether we realize it or not, we're always teaching our children something. That's why we need to heed what kind of example we set.

The quality and character of life we want to demonstrate to our children can be summarized by saying that those who know us best should be the ones who respect us the most. That is, as people (our children included) get to know us better and better, their respect for us should grow, not diminish.

There are a lot of well-known people in the world who, because of good public-relations work and television, are widely respected. But most people have only a superficial familiarity with these stars and celebrities. If we were to know those people in depth, however, and to see their priorities and how they treat others, our respect for them might diminish greatly. We would have to say of these people that those who know them best, respect them least. That's the opposite of what we want to be true for us.

The Bible gives us good illustrations of both kinds of people. For an example of someone who was respected most by those who knew him best, consider Noah. Here was a man given an amazing assignment by God, and for more than one hundred years he worked on that assignment, building "an ark for the salvation of his household" (Hebrew 11:7). God warned him that a flood was coming. His neighbors and countrymen didn't respect Noah much at all. Maybe they thought he was crazy. Whatever the case, they perished in the Flood. Indeed, if Noah were an evangelist, we would probably say he hadn't been a very effective one.

However, Noah wasn't called by God to be an evangelist to the world; he was called to build an ark for the salvation of his household. Most likely, working alongside him all those years were his wife, his sons, and his sons' wives. They got to know Noah pretty well.

A lot of things can go wrong during a building project like that. Smashed thumbs. Gopherwood board cut too short by a son who wasn't paying attention. You just can't fake your spirituality for long, let alone for one hundred and twenty years! People get to know you for what you really are!

But when the time came, and God told Noah to go into the boat, those seven people who knew him best followed him in his faith. There was a special relationship built up over all those years of working together. As a result, Noah's family had respect for him such that when he said the Lord had instructed them to enter the ark, they did so willingly, without argument (Genesis 7:1-7). They were saved.

Now imagine the typical father today in a situation of impending judgment. Ask yourself how his family would respond if he went home and said for the first time, "Honey, kids, a man told me today that God is going to judge the earth, but that He's also provided a way of salvation in Jesus Christ if we'll surrender our lives to Him. Then He'll take us to heaven and we won't have to be afraid of His judgment. So, come on; let's get down on our knees right now and pray." How many families would follow Dad's instructions and be saved? "Sure, Dad." Noah's family did.

There's no doubt that Noah's faith was great, and, in living it every day, he earned enormous respect from those who knew him best. But there is a deeper principle at work here. Noah didn't just spend more time with his family. They spent more time with him. He included them in his own life response to the Word of God that He had received. They walked with a wise man. The wise man didn't take time off to do whatever his children wanted to do. Tree houses are nice, but they weren't building a tree house. They were building an ark, and you can't hide an ark in your backyard.

The consequences of doing what is right in this world will eventually catch up with you. Some will mock you. You will miss a promotion or two. The socialites will mark you off the party list. Being faithful will cost you something. And when you have to take the heat for your stand, your children will be able to watch their parents endure the hardship of being true to their convictions. But it is in those moments that the fire of faith is handed down. The torch of God's Truth is passed from one generation to another, not during the good times, but in the heat of battle.

There are two ways in which we frustrate this process. One is by caving in to pressure and selling out before we have to suffer for our faith. We rationalize that God doesn't want us to be unhappy. So we compromise our way around every cross Christ would have us bear. There is not enough evidence to convict us of having convictions, and so we never feel the heat of persecution. Needless to say, our children have no desire to serve the God of a wimp. But there is another way we frustrate God's process of handing down faith.

In those cases where there is faithfulness, where convictions are tested by fire and found true, it is possible for our children to be elsewhere. When Dad and Mom take their stand, the kids are in school. They hear about it later. But it's never quite the same as being there and hearing your dad say, "I have to do what God requires of me." The country Gospel singers can make "mamma's prayers" sound like a cliche, but if you've ever heard a godly mother really pray in a time of crisis, you'd understand why those songs bring a tear to so many eyes. You can't stage these things for your children. Only God does. But if, like Noah, you have included your family in a lifestyle devoted to responding to God's warning, they will be there often enough to catch fire in the blaze of your personal convictions. It's a wonderful thing for a child to be able to say, "I respect my parents."

God uses the Bible stories to inspire us and to frighten us into obeying His commandments. Let's consider another father's example in a similar situation, on the eve of destruction, but this time with very different results.

Lot was a nephew of Abraham. When Abraham was called to leave all and follow God, Lot tagged along (Genesis 13:1-12). As the wealth of the two men increased in the land to which God had called Abraham, their herdsmen started getting in each other's way and arguing over the watering holes. So, to avoid further conflict, Abraham suggested that the two of them go their separate ways. He gave Lot his choice of where he wanted to go. Lot could choose between the fertile plains of the Jordan River and the hill country.

Making his decision based solely on economic consideration, Lot chose the plains of the Jordan where his sheep would have plenty of good grazing. The Bible says that, having parted from Abraham, Lot "pitched his tent toward Sodom." It was the Silicone Valley of shepherding. But the neighborhood was not a wholesome one.

Sodom and Gomorrah are infamous to this day for their sexual sin and perversion. But their primary sin was idleness and pride, brought on by great wealth (Ezekiel 16:48-49). They were very prosperous cities, and their money allowed them to grow lazy and to seek new ways to amuse themselves. Whenever that happens, people inevitably find their way into all kinds of perversion and sin; it has happened time and again throughout history.

You may know the story of what happened in Sodom and Gomorrah. God finally had enough of their sin, so He determined to destroy them as an example of His righteous judgment. In a conversation with Abraham, God promised to spare both cities if even ten righteous people resided there. Then the two angels departed for the wicked cities to take a census of the godly.

When the angels arrived at Sodom, they found Lot sitting in the gates of the city, probably trying to influence its course. Recall that the gates were the place of civil influence. Judges and elders sat in the gates. Lot realized that these "men" were not local residents, and he quickly ushered them into the protection of his house, but not in time to hide them from the homosexual mob in the city.

We get insight into Lot's character and reputation in what happened next. When the mob demanded that he turn the two guests over to them for their pleasure, Lot tried to offer them his two virgin daughters instead. (Thanks a lot, Dad!) Fortunately for the daughters, these men were not interested in women. They threatened Lot with rape, along with his guests.

At this point, one angel must have leaned over to the other and said, "I haven't counted ten yet. Have you counted ten?" Census completed, the angels pulled the two daughters back inside. They had seen enough. In fact, the whole town had seen enough, because the angels blinded them in a moment.

In the next scene (Genesis 19:12-17), the angels asked what seem to be some very odd questions.

"Whom else have you here?"

One basic hermeneutical principle is that God never asks questions just to gather information. He knows all the answers. I would also assume He briefs His angels when He sends them on a rescue mission. These angels were not just asking, "How many kids do you have? Any pets?" They were trying to bring a prodigal father back into touch with the real world. "Whom else have you here? A son-in-law?" This tells us that Lot had a married daughter somewhere in town. "And your sons." That is plural. There were at least two sons. "It's eleven o'clock, Lot. Do you know where your boys are tonight?" He didn't. "And your daughters (at least three, counting the married one and the two living at home). Bring them out of this place; for we are about to destroy this place."

It took as much faith for Lot to believe that these two "men" could destroy two great cities as it took for Noah to believe God could destroy the world with a flood. Both fathers were warned by God about things not yet seen.

So Lot quickly went to warn the fiancés of his two virgin daughters. "Up. Get out of this place for the Lord will destroy the city." But he appeared to his betrothed sons-in-law to be "jesting." Basically they were saying, "Come on, Lot. There you go again. Always trying to save the world. Just go home. Get some sleep. You'll get over it by morning."

So Lot went home. And when the morning dawned, the angels said, "Take your wife and the two daughters who are here and go." But Lot hesitated. Noah worked faithfully for some 120 years, but Lot couldn't make it through one night without doubting. Little wonder he was not a man respected most by those who knew him best. His sons-in-law were right. He got over it!

But aren't you glad you serve the God of Lot? Because the compassion of the Lord was upon him, the angels grabbed a hand of each family member and brought them out of the city. Our salvation does not depend on our own strength, but on God's grace. But, unfortunately, the story is not over yet.

You may be able to get your wife out of the city, but you may not be able to get the city out of your wife. As they were leaving, she looked back longingly at the comfortable metropolitan community she had grown to love, and God counted her unworthy. She was changed into a pillar of salt, a monument to the love of this world's pleasures.

You might also be able to get your daughters out of their age-segregated peer group, but it will be a little more difficult to get the peer group's influence out of your daughters. Later, in a cave, Lot's daughters realized that Dad was now the only man left in their lives. So they decided to get Dad drunk and seduce him, all in order to bear children by their father. Perhaps their motives were sincere. But a worthy end is used to justify an evil means. These two incestuous virgins conceived two boys, Ammon and Moab, founders of two tribes which would later be thorns in the side of Israel for hundreds of years.

Maybe they learned this kind of situational ethic in a Values' Clarification class at Sodom and Gomorrah High School. Or maybe they just learned it from their friends in the streets of the city. Either way, Lot's story is a sad one. One way or another, he had lost his family to the influence of an evil society. All of his social activism was in vain because he had neglected his family obligations.

And when we do a bit of arithmetic, we find a frightening possibility. When we add up the people just in Lot's immediate circle of influence, his wife, three daughters, at least two sons, two fiancés, a son-in-law, and himself, we have a minimum total of ten. Ten people. If Lot had devoted his time to being respected most by those who knew him best, both cities might have been spared. God said He would call off the destruction for the sake of ten righteous. Lot could have accomplished more for his community by simply taking better care of his own household.

However, even though the Genesis account doesn't give us a very flattering picture of Lot, the Apostle Peter described him as "righteous Lot" and said Lot "tormented his righteous soul from day to day by seeing and hearing their lawless deeds" (2 Peter 2:7-8).

Apparently Lot, living under the influence of godly Abraham, came to believe in the true and living God. But it also appears that his life and his works did not win the respect of others. He lost everyone and everything to the influence of Sodom. Only his own soul was saved, snatched like a brand from the burning.

Put simply, Lot was a man respected least by those who knew him best. He was the epitome of what we don't want to be. But the fact that Lot was still a righteous man should put a holy fear in our hearts. You can be righteous, saved, going to heaven, and still do some pretty foolish things with your family. Knowing God's Word is not enough. We must be doers of His Word, or else we're just deceiving ourselves. The Biblical basis for home schooling requires Biblical principles to be understood and obeyed from beginning to end.

Summary

As we've seen, the Bible gives us a clear mandate to educate our children. But it also gives us some guidelines on how to fulfill that calling, principles and precepts that enable us to confidently embark on the journey of a lifetime.

First of all, the educational mandate is directed at parents. No cop-outs allowed. "Train up a child in the way he should go, and when he is old he will not depart from it." That training isn't academic only, but also involves development of moral character, discipling our children for the Kingdom.

We need a Biblical way of understanding man in order to hold a Biblical understanding of education. Before all else, man is made in the image of God. He alone consciously blesses and worships God. Therefore, the task in education is for parents to prepare the next generation to fulfill God's purposes.

God also intends that our education should benefit the Church and society. Christ's Church needs strong families. Significantly, the Bible says if we would lead the people of God in church, we must first learn to lead them at home. Your family ought to be a model before your church and community.

Given these purposes of education, the Bible is given to illuminate the methods and the content of our instruction. For "All Scripture is given by inspiration of God, and is profitable for doctrine, for reproof, for correction, for instruction in righteousness, that the man of God may be complete, thoroughly equipped for every good work" (2 Timothy 3:16-17). Like regular mealtimes, Bible study should be part of our family routine.

Our opportunities to teach our children don't stop after those specific periods of Bible study, however. God expects parents to be sensitive to their children's needs for Christian understanding from sunrise to sunset.

In order to train our children in the way they should go, we as parents must ourselves be trained in that same way. We teach volumes by our example. Our children can detect what's most important to us without our ever saying a word.

The goal in parenting is to be respected most by those who know us best.

Noah stands as an example of such a father. His family found it easy to obey him. They were saved. Lot, on the other hand, got little respect from his family. He was a righteous man who lost his family to the surrounding culture.

The duty of Christian parents to impart a Christian education to their children is a tall order. Who is sufficient for these things? Only those who can say, along with the Apostle Paul, "I can do all things through Christ who strengthens me." (Philippians 4:13)

The great advantage of parent-directed tutoring is its philosophical dexterity, ambidexterity, and polydexterity. Soaring to the heights or swooping to the depths, it is free to be what 'ere they choose it to be.

Samuel Johnson

THE MODERN HOME SCHOOL MOVEMENT

Perhaps you've heard the story of the three blind men and the elephant. The three blind men, who had no idea what an elephant was like, one day came across one. The first man walked up to the beast and grabbed his trunk. "Aha!" he said, "I perceive that the elephant is very much like a snake."

The second man walked up and bumped into one of the pachyderm's legs. Feeling his way around the leg, he said, "You are wrong about the elephant, my friend. For I perceive that he is very much like a tree."

Then the third man walked up to the back of the beast and grabbing hold of the tail he said, "No, no, my friends, you're both wrong. Clearly, the elephant is very much like a rope." All three men then got into a long and loud argument, each insisting that his understanding of the elephant was correct.

Which man was right about the nature of elephants? Well, in one sense, they all were, but in another sense, none were. Each of them described accurately the particular part of the elephant he had encountered, but they all failed to consider that the elephant was made up of more than just the individual parts they had found.

In some ways, the modern home-school movement can be compared to an elephant. It's made up of many different parts, and if you only meet up with one of them, you might think that's all there is to it. In fact, however, it's a very diverse movement. Lest you think, then, that home schooling has only one shape, let's take a look at the many forms in which it comes.

Different Motivations

In the first place, not all parents who choose to school their children at home do it for the same reasons. Some, for example, are just concerned parents who recognize the inherent educational advantages of home schooling. They want one-to-one training and the ability to pace the process to the individual child's rate of progress. These parents might be agnostics or even atheists. And some of them are nominally religious, doing what they do for mainly secular reasons.

A second group of home-schooling parents are those who recognize that the public schools are working to destroy the religious values they, the parents, are trying to instill. This group might include any number of religious, but non-Christian, parents. It also includes parents who belong to the various religious cults. This group creates some tension in distinctively Christian home school support groups because they often want to be accepted as Christians, even though they know they are different. That is why they feel compelled to argue for their own doctrinal positions.

Finally, there are the evangelical Christian parents who want the educational advantages of home schooling and who want to give their children the training for all of life that the Bible calls on parents to provide. This is the largest and fastest-growing sector of the home-school movement (85 percent) and the best organized.

Different Time Frames

How long should the process of home schooling last? Some parents, this author included, believe in "total home schooling". That is, they intend to train their children from preschool through high school and even into college level. These parents believe the full responsibility for all aspects of their children's training is theirs from start to finish. Though we supplement our programs with outside courses and programs, from music lessons to local college courses, we intend to make learning a home-centered lifestyle that never ends.

A second approach is what author Mary Pride calls "transitional home schooling." The idea is that the first years of schooling should be done at home. ("First" is defined differently by each set of parents.) This training at home will give the child a head start, individual attention when they feel he most needs it and strong Christian teaching in his most impressionable years. Those who feel formal education should be avoided until eight to ten years of age fall into this group.

Eventually, however, these parents intend for their children to make the transition to formal schooling. This might come in the third grade or in junior high or at the beginning of high school, depending on what the parents think best. Many of these parents believe there are advantages to formal schooling that should not be overlooked entirely; others just can't see themselves schooling their children for thirteen years.

The third approach is what Pride calls "supplemental home schooling." Here, a child is enrolled in a formal school, either public or private, but the parents want to augment the education he receives there. Thus, the parents use evenings, weekends, vacations or special days off from school for further training for their child.

This is a form of home schooling that doesn't receive much publicity because it doesn't conflict with the common approach to education or with school attendance laws. It assumes the parents have no serious problem with the programs of the formal schools their children attend. They just want to add to what's being offered there. Most transitional home-schooling families switch to this approach once their children are enrolled in a formal school.

Supplemental home schooling is also a good intermediate step for parents who recognize the value of home education but aren't yet willing or able to make a full commitment.

Different Methods

As you might expect with these different *approaches*, there are also a number of very different *methods* of home schooling. The first of these is often called the "traditionalist model"; the parent, using a prepared curriculum, teaches the child as he would be taught in a formal classroom, giving him daily assignments, periodic tests, and so on. This is the method with which we're all familiar, especially if we went through the public school system. Some parents who use this method join an extension program through a local school, enrolling the child, receiving curriculum, sending in grades and coordinating activities with the school office. Others just buy a curriculum and use it strictly on their own. Though there is flexibility in the early years as to when and how certain subjects will be introduced and taught, there is a general consensus that teaching must be planned and enforced as a discipline. Traditional does not mean rigid.

In my experience, most of the leadership in the Christian home education associations across the United States and Canada are more or less traditional in their approach. As for myself, I ascribe to an approach that builds on the traditional methods but also leaves room for what I call "delight-directed" study. If you are a Christian with a Biblical view of child training, you will most likely feel at home with a group of traditionalist home-schooling families.

A second method, championed by the late John Holt and called "unschooling," moves far away from traditional schooling. Holt believed that children can learn by themselves and, thus, rejected most forms of programmed instruction. He argued that children will learn what they need to know if they're given the freedom to do so. In essence, his theory eliminates teaching as a profession, or even as a parental responsibility.

Holt's books offer a few helpful insights into how children learn and what's wrong with the public schools; for those views, they're worth reading. However, his basic assumptions about values and the nature of children ignore the effects of the Fall and, thus, are saddled with an untenable secular humanism. He was also an advocate for children's rights, which undermine parental authority.

A third method which is becoming increasingly popular with home schoolers is the "Unit Study" method. The value of a unit study is seen in the way it draws together many different areas of life into one integrated unit or topic of study.

One way to understand the difference between a conventional textbook approach and the unit study method is to imagine that the various subjects of study (e.g., language arts, science, history, geography, art, math, etc.) are colors of thread. A conventional lesson would examine each color in some degree of isolation from the others. "All right, children, it is time to study red thread. Take out your spool of red thread." The children take out their spool of red thread and begin to examine it carefully. When the bell rings for the next period it is time to study the blue thread. Its not difficult to see why children would find school boring.

In a unit study program we are still studying the various colors of thread (i.e., the subjects), but instead of looking at them in isolation, we focus on some small area of the larger tapestry of life to examine the colors in relation to the topic of our study. A unit study on the character quality of honesty might include reading the biography of George Washington, a model of honesty. It might include a brief activity related to auditing a company to check for honest bookkeeping, and perhaps it would even draw us into a report on the various laws that enforce honesty in various contexts, such as perjury in court and truth in advertising. The important thing is that the child sees the various subjects of study as part of life, not just part of school.

Unit studies are recommended by many respected home-school authors including Dr. Ruth Beechick, Valerie Bendt, Terri Lustig, Linda Hurst and others. Popular unit study materials include *Konos Curriculum*, based on character qualities, and *The Classics*, based on classic children's literature. Individual unit study guides for children's literature have also been developed by Ann Ward and others.

A sub-category of the Unit Study method is the Delight-Directed Unit Study. The main difference is seen in the way in which the topics of study are selected and developed by the teacher for the child. As the tapestry of life is spread before the child, some topics will be more interesting to him than others. A delight-directed study simply takes that fact into account. Because this principle is very important to our understanding of Christian education, we will explore it in the next chapter.

Summary

I realize that even after this look at the variety available in home schooling, and even after we've considered the advantages home schooling offers and the Biblical mandate to train our kids, you may still have questions and doubts about it or your ability to do it. And if that's true for you, read on. The next chapter seeks to answer the most common questions and objections about home schooling. But, for now, just remember:

Home schooling comes in all colors and shapes.

Motives differ.

People other than evangelical Christians who home school do so because of its obvious advantages, such as one-on-one training. Others of various religious persuasions want to instill their particular world-view into their children. Most evangelical Christian parents home school because of the educational and moral advantages. They believe God has given them this responsibility.

Time frames differ.

Some people think parents should home school their children from infancy to adulthood. Others believe in transitional home schooling, which allows children to stay home for the first few years of school to get a head start, individual attention when they need it most, and strong Christian teaching. A third approach is supplemental home schooling. Children attend a public or private school, but parents use weekends, evenings, and vacations as special times for further training. This makes a good intermediate step for parents who aren't quite ready to commit to home schooling.

Methods differ.

The traditionalist model resembles the formal classroom model without its rigidity. Parents use a prescribed curriculum; they give tests and daily assignments. Unschooling moves radically away from traditional schooling. According to advocates of this perspective, children will learn what they need to know when given the freedom to do so. Unit studies allow most studies to be organized around a theme (e.g. Honesty), or topic (e.g. Horses), or classic literature (e.g. Peter Rabbit), as an integrated unit that incorporates many different subject areas into one lesson plan.

Finally, delight-directed studies, based on the Biblical principle of delight, respond to the interests of each student in ways that make study more enjoyable while still providing parental oversight and accountability. This approach, which we will examine in detail in our next chapter, improves a child's ability to research areas of high interest and learn how to learn.

Together, these elements and many other subcategories make up the modern home-school movement. Together, they offer parents a wide range of options on how we can fulfill our God-given responsibilities.

A wise teacher makes learning a joy.

Proverbs 15:1 (Living Proverbs)

DELIGHT-DIRECTED STUDY

The young man sitting across from me seems to be speaking in a foreign language. He's saying something about "color plates" and "web runs" of so much per thousand. He sighs that the "trapping" wasn't right on the cover, so he has to order new proofs of the changes. Right.

Can this really be the same person who just a few short years before would give only polite attention to me as I showed him the glories of my new Macintosh computer complete with its revolutionary new Laserwriter printer? "Look at this; it's just like real type-setting!" I said. He wasn't interested, then. Now he's the publisher of a successful new magazine, while I sit here struggling to understand what in the world he's talking about. How did he learn so much so fast?

The young man is my son, Joshua, now twenty years old. The magazine is *New Attitude*, the national magazine for home-schooling teens. And the difference between that polite, but uninterested, adolescent back in 1987 and this enthusiastic young publisher is what this chapter is all about. It is the difference between conventional approaches to home education and delight-directed study.

Josh didn't show much interest in computers or publishing until he was sixteen. Before that time, he went through a series of interests. When he was thirteen, he was delighted with drawing cartoons. The result of that interest was our partnership in developing the coloring books in our three *House Rule Kits*.

When he was fifteen, he discovered our family video camera and became "the young movie director." We got some great family videos at that time, and all of my home-school seminars were captured on professional-quality videotape. Today, people in communities around the world view them whenever they choose (without my having to get on another airplane). Josh also earned good money videotaping family reunions and weddings. As long as he kept up with his other school assignments, we allowed him to put the rest of his time into building up his company, *Hizway Video Productions.* He was having a great time.

At that point we thought he might make video work his career. But after attending The National Conference of Professional Wedding Videographers, he changed his mind. He met the best in the field and came away knowing that it was not what God wanted him to do with his life. It was an expensive decision because he owned a lot of equipment, but we were glad he came to his conclusion early, rather than waiting until he had a wife and children to feed.

Soon after that, Josh announced that he would like to try his skills as a public speaker. He had always done a good job working up skits for his youth group at church, so I made arrangements for him to speak for one forty-five minute session in my next Portland workshop.

Josh prepared for his first presentation as though it were the State of the Union Address. He read books on public speaking. He made overhead transparencies. He used extensive written notes. He timed his talk down to the last minute. He practiced for weeks.

Imagine a sixteen-year old speaking to a crowd of about four hundred parents on the topic, *Why Home School Through High School?* He told his own story of wanting to get out of home schooling at age thirteen, and why he was glad his dad and mom stood firm and continued to teach him at home. It was a good speech, and because he was also still a videographer, he had arranged to videotape his debut as a speaker. The speech and the video were so well done (and we had so many requests for copies of the tape) that we decided to go ahead and publish it.

That decision created the occasion for Josh's first real interest in desktop publishing. You see, we needed to design the cover for his video tape, and it was his "baby," so it had to be done just right. Needless to say, his artistic juices began to flow and, lo and behold, he discovered he actually enjoyed using the Macintosh to lay out that cover: picking the fonts, scanning the photos, picking the paper stock and even dealing with the printer. An important seed was sown, one which would come up later.

A year later, after Josh had traveled with me several times, spoken in a few more events and met a few hundred like-minded home-school teens across the U.S. and Canada, the idea came to him for a magazine that would address the needs of such teens. As Josh put it, "A magazine that will challenge home schoolers to reach their full potential for Jesus Christ." After much prayer and consultation, the project was launched. And just as with his public speaking, Josh's delight was the rocket fuel. His mind was like a sponge.

In a matter of months, this seventeen-year old had mastered the complicated techniques of computer graphics and understood the subtle effects of font combinations. Designing each page became a science and an art. He studied the layouts of every magazine that caught his eye. Though graphic design continued to be his passion, he also rose to the challenge of mastering the mundane details of publishing and delivering a magazine: dealing with the printing industry, setting up his bookkeeping system, designing a database for his subscribers, and a dozen other disciplines. Everything related to his magazine became the most interesting things in the world.

Now, three years later, after putting out nine issues of *New Attitude Magazine*, conducting five teen conferences and receiving nearly four thousand subscriptions, it appears that Josh is more delighted than ever. And his younger brother, Joel, now twelve years old, has become his delighted sidekick.

What Is Going On Here?
A delight-directed study is like a wonderful fire in the mind of a student. It starts small, but as it grows, it begins to consume vast amounts of information until it bursts into a roaring blaze of insight, understanding and creativity. It takes on a life of its own.

In a delight-directed study, a child's interests are fanned to flame and supported in ways that increase his interest in his studies. The child's delight is the spark that ignites everything. Once established, like a fire, it is self-sustaining. The student begins to study for his own personal satisfaction, and the fruits of his study begin to flow outward to others.

This approach is especially helpful for the child who has been "burned out" on school. It helps restore his love for learning. But delight-directed study is more than just a method of remedial instruction. As we shall see, it is the foundation for all true scholarship. Once the basic concepts of delight are understood, the approach itself is easy to implement.

Is This Anything Like Unschooling?

At first glance, delight-directed study, with its emphasis on enjoying study, may sound a bit like the unschooling approach mentioned earlier. Unschooling, developed by the late education reformer and author, John Holt, emphasizes the child's freedom from adult control. It takes a more or less non-directive approach toward instruction. Like Rousseau, Holt viewed adults, and especially parents, as the major defilers of children. The result of his liberal bias abandons children to their own limited resources and further disarms parents in the face of child rebellion. There is little place for discipline in unschooling.

Delight-directed study is child-responsive, but still parent-supervised. Dad and Mom remain fully in charge, and discipline is a constant part of the mix. Delight-directed study strategies are more responsive to the interests of the student, without being indulgent. Rather than allow the student to study whatever he sees fit, however he sees fit, delight-directed study urges parents to guide their child's studies and establish clear accountability for his work. Also, whereas unschooling is deeply humanistic and therefore disdainful of the Scriptures, delight-directed study is based on a distinctively Christian worldview and has substantial support in the Bible.

God is Good

The foundation for delight-directed study is the doctrine of the *Goodness of God*. While most of us agree that God is good, we may not realize just what that means to our day-to-day experience. But the Bible is clear that God is good.

"Praise the LORD. Give thanks to the LORD, for he is good; his love endures forever" (Psalms 106:1, Ps. 107:1, 118:1, 118:29, 136:1).

"How can I repay the LORD for all his goodness to me?" (Psalm 116:12).

The word *good* means "beneficial." A good God does everything He does for good reason. That means there are real benefits in every aspect of God's activity. When God observed, in the first chapter of Genesis, that everything He had made was good, it meant that everything served a good purpose.

Unfortunately, we live in a fallen world. Things are not entirely the way God intended them to be. Thorns and weeds choke out the good fruit God intended to grow. There is an element of pain involved in childbirth that is not good. Because of Adam's sin, evil has come into what was a perfect world, and bad things now happen along with the good. The hearts of all people have been corrupted. We are all "the bad guys," and no one is good enough to save himself. That is why we need a Savior. God, in His never-ending goodness, has provided such a Savior by sending His own Son to die for our sins. That is the "good news."

If you have never understood this before, put your faith in Jesus now. Ask God to forgive you, for Jesus sake, and help you to turn away from your sin. By doing so, you will be born again into God's eternal family. For those of us who have believed in Jesus, a great deal more of God's goodness is made available. The Apostle Paul tells us in Romans 8:28 that "in all things God works for the good of those who love him, who have been called according to his purpose." In Christ we have eternal, spiritual salvation. But we also enjoy substantial shelter from the effects of Adam's sin. By our obedience to God's Word, we can avoid many of the sorrows that come to those who continue to live in rebellion against God. When Christ returns, God's justice will be established once and for all, without challenge. Everything will be put right. Everything will be totally and completely good again.

Fortunately, the Fall of Man did not erase all of the goodness of God's original design in creation. It still peeks through. When we look past the many imperfections, we can see His goodness still on display. One tell-tale sign of this is that whenever an activity is necessary, it also brings us wholesome pleasures. Whatever is *needed,* is also *enjoyable.* That simple fact is evidence of the goodness of God in His design for man. Consider a few examples.

We need sleep. God allows our sleep to be refreshing. We must have sight. God allows us to see in beautiful *color,* even though most animals cannot do so. We need our sense of smell. God allows us to enjoy sweet fragrances. We must hear. God allows us to enjoy music. We must eat. God allows wholesome foods to taste good, and He has provided various spices to improve on what He has already made. We get thirsty. God has provided cool, refreshing water. We need to exert these wonderful bodies God has given us. We need exercise. As difficult as it may be for some to believe, God allows us to experience exhilaration in doing hard work, playing active sports and even in something as simple as running or walking. We must procreate. Our good God allows us to rejoice in the intimacy we have with our spouses. In the bonds of holy matrimony, such intimacy is intended to be enjoyable, without shame or regret. That is why our young people need the protection and support of family and community standards to keep them from spoiling the good things God holds in store for them in marriage.

Ultimately, as I mentioned before, we are *homo adorans,* "worshipping man," and we must worship God. It is our nature to do so. Human beings are incurably religious. No other animal shares this human trait. If ever there would be an occasion where compulsion, and even our discomfort, would be utterly appropriate, this would be it. God is worthy of our praise whether we feel like praising Him or not, and whether we enjoy praising Him or not. And yet, in praise and worship we find the greatest of all benefits, for in the presence of the Lord there is joy! (Ps. 16:11, Ps. 21:6 & Acts 2:28) Our God is indeed a GOOD God.

"Praise the LORD, O my soul, and forget not all his benefits—who forgives all your sins and heals all your diseases, who redeems your life from the pit and crowns you with love and compassion, who satisfies your desires with good things so that your youth is renewed like the eagle's" (Psalms 103:2-5).

But when it comes to schooling our children, we Christians doubt God's goodness. In a fit of uninformed conservatism, we bring out the "hickory stick" and demand that our students submit to their instruction without regard for their enjoyment or pleasure. School attendance is compulsory. Teachers must be stern and mean. We suspect that something must be wrong if our students are actually enjoying their studies, because we didn't. "It's not supposed to be fun," we say. "Studying is a discipline."

Is it really? Granted, children need discipline for their disobedience, and they are as likely to disobey in school as anywhere else. And there is, of course, a general need for self-discipline in their studies, just as there is in their development of skills in music, art or sports. But nowhere else do we find it necessary to make everything so joyless and compulsory. In every other area of human need, the wholesome pleasure of satisfying what is needed draws the person into the activity.

Why is there so much emphasis on teaching young people to endure hour after hour of boring, disjointed and generally uninteresting activity? Why is schooling such a deadening experience for so many, even in high school and college? Is it possible that the main objective of our school system, with its passion for responding to school bells, blindly following instructions, and fitting in to the social pecking order, is not academic at all, but rather preparation for the labor force? Could this be the education of pawns?

John Taylor Gatto, former New York City and New York State "Teacher of the Year," in his foreword to *Government Nannies* by Cathy Duffy, believes it to be so. He suggests that our modern, forced schooling started in Prussia in 1819 where the clear goal of free public education was to deliver obedient soldiers to the army and obedient workers to the mines and factories. Times have not changed. Our free, compulsory, government-regulated education system is still a tool of social engineering. Even our most recent school "reform bills," such as Goals 2000, have been advanced under the banner of maintaining national competitiveness in the emerging international economy. The goal is now to deliver global citizens as employees for the multinational corporations. Students in such a system are more likely to be exploited than to be served.

But having withdrawn from the compulsory system, we must beware not to bring its labor force agendas home. A media communications philosopher in the 1970s announced that "The medium IS the message." In other words, the *way* we receive our information (or education) overwhelms the content of what we receive. The attitudes and assumptions of the conventional schools, public and private, are more powerful than the content of their curricula. The schools' structures and methods reflect the purposes for which they were established, whether it be to create soldiers, laborers, or whatever. Their purposes may be noble or ignoble, but that tells us nothing about the nature of learning itself. What is the nature of learning?

The answer to this question is based, not on tradition or technology or politics, but on the character of God. When it comes to our basic need to study, is God still good? Is what is needed also enjoyable in this case? The answer is, "Yes, He is good." And, in fact, God allows our studies to be *delightful*.

Study is a Delight

If the Goodness of God is the foundation for delight-directed study, the pillars of the edifice are found in the way the word "delight" is used in Scripture.

But his delight is in the law of the LORD, and on his law he meditates day and night (Ps. 1:2).

Great are the works of the LORD; they are pondered by all who delight in them (Ps. 111:2 NIV). (Or, "by all who find pleasure in them" KJV).

Praise the LORD. Blessed is the man who fears the LORD, who finds great delight in his commands (Ps. 112:1).

I delight in your decrees; I will not neglect your word (Ps. 119:16).

The large crowd listened to [Jesus] with delight (Mark 12:37).

For in my inner being I delight in God's law (Rom. 7:22).

Over and over in God's Word, we find that the word "delight" is closely associated with different aspects of study. Pondering, listening, meditating, reading, etc., are all activities that bring delight. There is no need for coercion in any of them. Occasionally we find the idea of delight expressed without the specific word itself: "How sweet are your words to my taste, sweeter than honey to my mouth!" (Ps. 119:103).

The English language has been watered down by misuse over the years. The word "delight" is defined in modern dictionaries as little more than a synonym for joy. But Bible scholar James Strong, author of *Strong's Exhaustive Concordance*, in 1890 noted that the Hebrew word for "delight" denotes "pleasure related to some matter of value to the mind." Noah Webster, in his 1828 dictionary, defines "delight" as "...a high degree of pleasure or satisfaction of mind. A delight," writes Webster, "is a more permanent pleasure than joy, and is not dependent on sudden excitement." These men studied the English language and understood its subtle shades of meaning.

According to their definitions, a delight is a pleasurable and relatively permanent state of mind. For our purposes, that word "permanent" is important. If it is more or less permanent, we can count on a delight still being there *tomorrow*. It is not just another passing interest.

When a child begins to refer to an interest over and over again for several days, ("Look, Mom, there's ANOTHER horse!") that child may be developing a "delight." Because of its ability to bring pleasure to his mind and its relative permanence, you can incorporate it into your lesson plans. It's like discovering your child likes a certain type of vegetable; you can make sure to serve that vegetable more often in the future.

This suggests that the human mind has an appetite for certain knowledge, just as the body has an appetite for certain foods. Whereas our palates yearn for something "delicious," our minds hunger for something "delightful." This is the key metaphor by which to understand delight-directed studies.

According to this idea, a well-prepared lesson will be like a feast for your child's mind.

Let's consider the implications of this metaphor and see whether or not the relationships make sense. First, to prepare a delightful course of study, we would view our curricula and reference materials as a set of cookbooks and a pantry full of wholesome ingredients. Our goal is to prepare balanced meals. But food left on the plate goes to waste. So we have to make the meal taste as good as we can. To do so, our presentations should make use of what we know to be our student's established tastes. It would not be enough to simply say, "This is good for you, so just learn it." We must make the information more appetizing by the way we introduce it and present it. We might explain how the new information relates to something else we know he has enjoyed in the past, and we may need to spice up some items that would otherwise be unappealing.

In the early stages of a child's training, we will have to spoon-feed him. Later, with a few basic skills like reading and writing and simple arithmetic, he should be able to feed himself, under our close supervision. As he grows more confident, he will be able to prepare his own lessons, especially on those topics that he enjoys most. He may even begin to shop the libraries and bookstores for his own study resources. Eventually, he will want to prepare meals for the minds of others.

Certainly there are many things that children have to acquire a taste for, and some may be difficult to prepare in an interesting way. Try as we will, some things will simply never be delightful. In those cases, if it really is important, we may require that a small portion be consumed, whether he likes it or not. But we know from experience that if we cram too much of anything down our student's throat, so to speak, it will become all the more distasteful to him. Time and maturity will affect his tastes. On the other hand, though there is no harm in serving a little dessert now and then, we must be careful not to fill our child's mind with the mental equivalent of junk food and candy through television or computer games.

Our metaphor stands up well, provided we don't try to take it too far. We are free to prepare a feast for our child's mind. Because we are responding to a natural need in his life, a real appetite, we can be confident that he will come looking for something to feed his mind. As home-schooling parents, we can be ready for him with good things that satisfy his delight.

The Power of Companionship

Where do delights come from? The answer raises the issue of socialization, which we discussed briefly in an earlier chapter. At this point we only consider the larger implications of Proverbs 13:20. "Those who walk with the wise become wise, but a companion of fools will suffer harm." God's Word, we are told, is sharper than any two-edged sword. In this case, it cuts both ways. Our companions will either do us good, or do us harm.

Whether wise or foolish, there is a clear relationship between companionship and the delights we choose to study. Simply put, we study whatever delights us, and we easily become delighted in that which our companions delight in. In a sense, we "catch" our delights from others. Sports heroes, musicians and other entertainers have a profound effect on the young in our nation. National fads in music, toys and clothing sweep the country by means of celebrity endorsements and word-of-mouth recommendations. Such "companionship" wields a powerful influence.

But so does the private companionship of parents and siblings. As parents, we must consider the quality of the companionship our children have with us and with other family members and friends. Our own interests and delights are easily transferable. If we enjoy reading, we can share that delight with our children. Be it gardening, prayer, cooking, smoking, sewing, car repair, Bible study, drinking, fishing, hunting or any other interest, it's all contagious. Older siblings also bring influences into the lives of their younger brothers and sisters. The neighborhood kids bring a mixed bag of potential, as well. Everyone is a carrier of one delight or another.

So beware. For good or ill, a mature, enthusiastic delight is extremely contagious. This is where God's Word cuts to the heart of the matter. Foolish companions will induce one another to try out and ultimately to "study" foolish delights. Skateboarding and computer games come to mind. So do drugs and alcohol. Though some activities comprise only a waste of time, others result in an incredible loss of life. Our children will pursue whatever their companions are delighted in.

This is not a pitch for keeping little Johnny away from "those kinds of people." The "wrong crowd" is all around us. So is the right crowd. Wise and foolish are found in every social, economic, racial, ethnic and, yes, even religious category. Foolishness is pandemic, and wisdom is far too rare. In our efforts to protect our children from foolish companions and guide them toward better companions, we have to accept a general truth: the age of their companions makes a big difference. The Bible tells us that foolishness is bound up in the heart of a child, and only by firm and consistent discipline will that foolishness be driven out. That means, the older and more disciplined their companions are, the more likely they are to be wise. Spending most of their time with pals their own age is not a good idea, no matter what age they are. Walking with the older people in their lives is the only path to greater wisdom.

In the Vol. 1, No. 4, 1993 issue of *New Attitude Magazine*, my son Josh reports the sad story of a group of home-school teens from good, Christian families who began to drink beer after their weekly home-school basketball practices and games. Over a three-year period, they got into drinking in a big way. What started out as a lark became a disaster, as several teens became full-fledged alcoholics. One young man left home and is still drinking heavily. He has not finished high school and has trouble keeping a job.

How could such a thing happen? Where were their parents? They were just like you or I would be in this kind of situation. These were older teens. It never occurred to them that this might happen. These were "good" kids from "good" families.

Josh's point in recounting this embarrassing story is to warn parents and teens of the mistake in thinking there are no opportunities for home-school kids to ruin their lives. It could just as easily have been drug abuse or pornography or sex or the occult. "Not in my family!" you say. Companionship, even in the most godly of settings, can do harm if the companions are foolish.

Wisdom normally comes with age and experience (though not always). Therefore, age mates are almost always the companions of fools to some degree. The drinking pals were too close in age to do one another much good. As one of the boys reports it, "It wasn't one person leading everyone down the tubes; it was all of us encouraging each other." No one had the seniority to say, "Hey, guys, this is wrong." Their social life was too age-segregated.

The only effective precaution is to keep the older and younger people together as much as possible. The old-fashioned chaperone is not enough. Young people need to walk *with* the wise, not just be guarded by them. That means doing more of what the older members of the family enjoy doing. The old-fashioned barn dance was not chaperoned. Everyone was there, young and old alike. The result was a lot more wholesome and fun.

In an age-integrated setting, the delights of the older, wiser members of the family are the focal point. Wholesome pleasures are passed down to the younger members of the family. Rather than watching the youngsters do their thing and intervening only when they start to do something illegal or dangerous, we have to take the kids with us where we want to go. They learn to enjoy what we enjoy. Rather than taking a day off from our work to spend some time with the children at an amusement park, we would all be better off if we let them take a day off from their school or play to spend the day with us. They need to be with us as we do whatever we normally do.

Wise companions can impart their delights to others, just like any other companions. They, too, radiate their enthusiasm and become contagious. The difference will be in the worthiness of the topics of their delight and in the strategies by which they pursue their studies. The activities should be enjoyable. You don't have to be a nerd or a stick-in-the-mud just because you are grown up. But there will be a balance in the activity. More work than play, occasional breaks, refreshment and plenty of lively conversation to keep the time together from becoming boring. We don't have to entertain our children if we will just include them.

Often, the youngster's delight arises out of his own experience and then receives encouragement and assistance from the wise people in his life. Joshua's interest in art was a delight that took hold primarily as he showed his cartoons to his mother and me. Our enthusiastic response fed his interest. When I took him to an art-supply store and invested in a few good pens, his delight in art took off quickly, and his skills improved dramatically.

When my second son, Joel, began to show an interest in piano, we responded again as an appreciative audience. There is more to this than just an occasional compliment. When I picked up a music book that I knew Joel would enjoy, it told him I cared about his music. When we changed to a piano teacher who had a record of making music more enjoyable and producing more delighted students, it helped Joel see his music as more than just another discipline. When we all show up at his annual recitals, it reminds him of the way we used to all go to Josh's gymnastics meets. It says, "we think this is important." Every family has to make choices as to where it will put its money. As I write this, we happen to have the ugliest old couch you could ever imagine. When we scraped together the money to buy Joel a synthesizer and software for his computer so that he could get involved in music composition, it showed him that we are excited about the effort he puts into practicing. Some day we will buy a new couch. But right now our children's delights take priority.

The key here is that we are our children's wise companions. Even though neither my wife nor I can draw or the play piano well, we were an appreciative audience; and we had the ability to support Josh and Joel in their endeavors. Whether parent to child or sibling to sibling or friend to friend, wise companions will inspire one another to greater excellence in the interests they share.

As Your Own Poets Have Said

Thus far, I have focused my comments on the positive companionship of family members, and the negative companionship of age mates outside the family. I have said nothing about the potential of walking with wise people beyond your household.

God has given us the entire world as a source of his goodness. Every human being has something good to offer because God created him. In the light of God's Word, everything is here for our enjoyment. I believe great ideas, great art, great music, great literature, great films and great plays can all be enjoyed with proper Christian discretion. The Apostle Paul saw fit to quote pagan poets in his Sermon on Mars Hill (see Acts 17:28) saying, "For in him we live and move and have our being. As some of your own poets have said, We are his offspring!" Paul must have studied at least some of the literature of his day. In our quest to protect our children from evil, we must be careful that we do not impoverish their cultural heritage. Some parents will not allow any art or music or literature, for fear that some harm may come of it. I admire their caution, but I question their strategy.

The Bible warns us not to call good, evil, or evil, good. Some parents are unwilling to sort out the good from the evil, and so they try to toss out the entire culture! That won't work. Our kids will see through it, and we will lose their respect. If all we ever do is build fences around our children, our children will learn how to climb fences. If we teach our children by our own good example how to have good taste and how to maintain the standards of a strong Biblical conscience, we will not have to serve as their gate-keepers forever. They must see us enjoying the good things in life as people with discriminating tastes and high moral standards. Otherwise, they may write off our entire lifestyle as religious legalism and anti-intellectualism. For every evil thing we decide to reject, we should look for something good to support. For every fence we put up to keep our children away from something, we should try to put in a sidewalk to guide their footsteps toward the good things God has given us to enjoy. In the culture wars, as with any other conflict, the best defense is a good offense.

Sitting at the Feet of Solomon

There is another aspect to delight-directed study that is clearly Biblical, and that, I believe, deserves our careful attention. I am speaking of our ability to seek out and meet the leaders in any field of study. Whatever your delight may be, there is someone out there who has achieved excellence in pursuing it. Identify those people, locate them, write to them, call them up, invite them over or go visit them if at all possible. That is the strongest and most powerful expression of the power of companionship, one which Christ Himself honored.

In Luke 11:31, our Lord compliments the initiative of a pagan queen, while serving a powerful indictment on the religious leaders of His day. "The Queen of the South will rise at the judgment with the men of this generation and condemn them; for she came from the ends of the earth to listen to Solomon's wisdom, and now one greater than Solomon is here." The unstated observation is that the proud Pharisees and Sadducees would not even cross the street to hear the greater wisdom of Christ Himself. The Queen of Sheba was a delight-directed student with a willingness to travel. Being a sovereign with a high interest in issues of government policy, she had to come and see for herself the glory of Solomon's kingdom. She was not disappointed.

When I was getting started in my work of presenting seminars, I had the opportunity to meet Bruce Wilkinson, founder of *Walk Thru The Bible Ministries*. Dr. Wilkinson looms high above me in my field. The quality of everything he does amazes me. His seminars are state-of-the-art. When he agreed to have dinner with me while in Portland, it was exciting. Here was someone who understood everything I was going through because he had been through it himself. Every suggestion he made was right on target. By listening to his counsel and following through with his advice, I know I have avoided having to learn many lessons the hard way.

But even beyond the specific advice he gave, was the intense awareness that I was talking to a man who, within the field of Christian education, is a giant. It may sound silly, but he was like Solomon to me; and I was like the Queen of the South, sitting there listening. I know he is "just a man." But shaking his hand set a number of things in motion in my life. Dr. Wilkinson is, in a sense, my hero. I had shaken his hand, and now it was time to put my hand to the task of trusting God in my own life's work.

Josh shared a similar story in one of his conferences concerning Joel Belz, founder and publisher of *World Magazine*. I had received a call that Mr. Belz was going to be in our area. Having met him on other occasions, I called to see if he would like to join my family for dinner while he was in town. I hadn't really thought of it as anything extraordinary, because at that point there was no magazine publishing on the horizon for our family. But God had more in mind than I realized.

Josh stayed at the table after dinner to listen to the stories of how Mr. Belz got started in publishing, how his own father, as a pastor, had bought an old printing press for the church and how he had grown up with printer's ink under his fingernails. When he got to the part where he launched *World Magazine*, another seed was sown in Josh's heart. "So that's how great things get started," Josh thought to himself. A year later, the idea for *New Attitude Magazine* was presented. Unbeknownst to me, the power of companionship, through our hospitality, had left its mark again.

As time and opportunity allow, I try to introduce my children to the most inspiring people in their chosen fields. It may be something as simple as taking Joel to the concert of a gifted musician (and perhaps waiting around afterward to shake hands and get his autograph), or it might be as elaborate as helping Josh participate in Billy Graham's Evangelists' Training Conference in Puerto Rico. At age nineteen, Josh sat at the feet of every major evangelist in the world for one intense week. His heroes are men like Ravi Zacharius, Leighton Ford, Luis Palau and, of course, Billy Graham. Sometimes the encounter has the opposite effect. When Josh met some of the greatest wedding videographers in the world, his response was, "Why don't these guys get a life?!" It extinguished his interest in climbing any higher on that particular ladder.

I will do whatever it takes to allow my children to catch a good case of the delight that has made their godly heroes great. Not every musician, no matter how talented, is a worthy candidate to play the role of Solomon in my child's life. Not every minister of the gospel is a good role model either. But there are many who qualify in every legitimate field, and I will do my best to find them and help my children meet them.

Iron on Iron

Sometimes companions don't immediately recognize one another's greatness until much later. Sometimes it is their intense, and even combative, companionship that helps to make them great. "As iron sharpens iron, so one man sharpens another" (Prov. 27:17).

An odd collection of aspiring Christian authors used to meet in the back corner of an English pub to read their latest prose to one another. After each one read, they would sharpen their skill of literary criticism. By some reports, they didn't often enjoy one another's work. C.S. Lewis thought J.R. Tolkien seemed ashamed of the Gospel. Tolkien was repulsed by Lewis's apparent need to wear his faith on his sleeve. Dorothy Sayers' early works were judged to be too stiff and cold, much like the corpses she would leave lying about so freely in her famous murder mysteries. They were amateurs and wannabes with raw, unpolished gifts. They called themselves "The Inklings." Looking back, we see now that they were coals of creative fire radiating one another's glow in the amazing power of companionship. From their delight-directed enclave sprang some of the greatest English authors in history. Could they have known? Probably not. Neither can we know today what God is brewing in our early friendships. That is why we should never despise the day of small things—or small ones. Once delight-directed study takes root, great things are sure to be in store.

Once companions settle on an area of mutual interest, they will give themselves tirelessly to researching it as best they can. They will develop new skills, gather new information, identify the "Solomons" in their field of delight, and meet regularly to present to one another the results of their efforts.

Conventional "hickory stick" teachers are too quick to call this sort of study a distraction. They demand that their students quit the fun and games and get back to their studies. But I believe this kind of study is the true garden of excellence. Delight is the flower of companionship. Study is its pleasant fragrance. And either wisdom or foolishness will be its fruit. We will know the tree by its fruit. If it is rooted in walking with the wise, its fruit should be very good.

Waiting for the Bud to Open

The great virtue on the part of parents and other teachers in all of this may be patience. We want so much for our children to be good students who earn good grades and go on to do good things. But coercion to study is not likely to create a taste for good things in our students. Remember that discipline is the proper response to your child's disobedience, but not necessarily to his boredom. Boredom itself is a sign of his unsatisfied mental hunger. If you want him to study, feed his mind, don't punish him for being hungry.

Impatient attempts to force a student to learn something that holds no interest for him may be like trying to pry open the petals of a rosebud. You may be able to get them open, but the result won't be very pretty. Good study habits are more likely to be established through pleasant experiences with study, not by threats and punishments.

Pleasant experiences in study are not the same as doing what comes easy. If studies are too easy, they become boring. If they are too difficult, they become frustrating. The right degree of difficulty, followed by success, is exhilarating. The challenge for you, as a teacher, is to monitor the level of difficulty to be sure the studies remain interesting. Victory is pleasant to the mind.

Pleasant experience in study also requires relevance. The question of how something relates to anything the student cares about should be answerable. For example, no one I know reads just for the sake of reading, without regard for the usefulness or relevance of the content. No one counts just for the sake of counting. We count something. If we are counting our own allowance, it makes the numbers more relevant and interesting. If we are measuring the boards for our treehouse or fort, it makes the measurements interesting. Without relevance, all study is likely to be boring.

The first time I tried to get Josh to learn how to use my desktop publishing software, he went through the motions, but as soon as we were done, he was out of there. His heart was not in it—yet. He had nothing he wanted to publish. Today, as a publisher, he sometimes wishes he had learned these skills earlier in his life.

But I wonder if his doing so might not have had the opposite effect. Music lessons too early can cause some children to grow weary with their instruments before they have the maturity to play them well. Premature exposure to competition in sports can kill all desire to be an athlete (as many a sports-nut father has discovered the hard way). Prying open the bud is a bad idea. Just set the stage for the flower to open by itself. Rest in the knowledge that God is good, and that time is on your side.

Launching Your Student Like a Rocket

The implications of delight-directed study are wonderful, but what can we actually do with it? The answer may seem vague to some, but these ideas are like the atmosphere we breath. They should permeate and affect everything we do, but they don't require us to do everything differently. We may do many of the same things, but for different reasons and with a stronger sense of how each relates to our goals as teachers.

Should we throw away our textbooks and grade level materials? No. Good textbooks, like good cookbooks, are very useful reference materials. In some subjects, like math, we may find it best to use them as they were designed to be used. For other subjects, like science, history and literature, we may treat them like topical extensions of our encyclopedia sets. Their illustrations and explanations can be brought out whenever we need to present a skill or an idea related to our unit studies and study projects.

How you approach each lesson or study project should be affected by the level of instruction for which your child is ready. Think of it as launching a three-stage rocket to the stars. The first stage is lift-off. The second stage is achieving a stable orbit. And the third stage is the final thrust that takes your student out of orbit and toward his final destination. These three stages correspond roughly to the elementary grades where basic skills and rules are the dominant focus, the junior high grade level where everything is pivotal and tentative, and, finally the senior high grade levels where adulthood, career, marriage and family are in view.

There is no line drawn in our children's minds that says, "Now you are in junior high school or high school." It is NOT a matter of AGE. This is because a child who is delighted in something will race past grade level very quickly in that area and yet lag behind in those areas that do not hold his interest. We could just as easily use a child's shoe size, as his age, to decide his grade level.

Rather than basing our decisions of study level on a student's age, it is better to consider the student's attitude and ability. Higher grade levels generally offer greater liberty for the student to design his own courses of study. He will be more independent. The question is, has he earned this privilege by his past performance? Does he honor and obey his parents? Can he be trusted to use his freedom faithfully by staying on his assignments when we are not watching? Greater liberty should only be given to those students who have been consistently faithful in the past.

The second question is one of ability. Is the student ready to go into higher levels of study? Can he do the work? Has he developed the requisite skills and general knowledge? Are there major holes and gaps in his understanding? Various written and oral tests can help us answer these questions. More difficult are the questions of emotional readiness. Can he handle higher levels of material? Some social studies topics are frightening and depressing. Some bright students cannot cope with what they understand. Some cannot deal with the pressures of a rigorous schedule of school assignments. These are the questions that should decide a student's graduation into the next grade level, and certainly from elementary into junior high, and from junior high into senior high.

But regardless of grade level, the fuel that drives all three stages of this rocket is our child's delights. Let's take a quick look at each launch stage of delight-directed study.

ELEMENTARY SCHOOL: At this stage you are your child's *Coach* in the *Game of Life*. As a good coach, you will be training him in all the skills and teaching him all the rules he needs in order to play the games of reading, writing, arithmetic, spelling, grammar, etc. In addition to the basic skills and rules, he can begin to pick up general knowledge about various topics in history, geography and social studies. At this stage a good student will be *receptive*. The rules are the rules. Debate comes later. Reading instruction, field trips and what my wife calls "kitchen math" can suffice in the first few grades. Reading together covers a lot of territory. But how can you get a student at this level to apply himself to his studies and learn all these rules?

The answer is: through the power of your companionship. If those your child loves and admires are reading to him and with him, and if they are concerned about spelling and grammar, etc., their concerns for these things will be planted in your child as well. He will want to learn how to play these games with you! It is the relationship that makes these activities delightful. The skills and rules are just part of the game. Once your child has these basic skills established, he will need lots of practice, and that is where a good study project becomes so practical.

The key is in picking *what* your child will practice *on*. When I buy a new woodworking tool, like a jig saw, I need to learn how to use it. I don't waste expensive wood cutting curlicues. I use a piece of scrap wood. Its value is only as something to practice on.

So relax. Don't be too picky about what your child practices his new skills on. A delight in frogs or dogs is a great opportunity to strengthen reading, writing and presentation skills. They will also teach your child how to study. When your child begins to show an enduring interest in anything that is wholesome or, at least, harmless, you can respond to it with a delight-directed study strategy. It is a spark that you hope to fan into a flame. You don't have to develop a formal unit study. It can be just a study project, like making a scrapbook about baseball. But when the delight comes into full bloom, you may want to organize a full-scale unit study around it. For an example of a delight-directed unit study at the elementary level, let's consider the topic of baseball.

A child with basic reading skills and a high interest in baseball can be assigned to read biographies of the great ballplayers in various periods of American history. He will live through American history through the eyes of baseball's all-time greats. When World War I breaks out in Europe during one player's career, your child will probably want to know what they were fighting about. Look it up in your encyclopedia; answer his questions; then get back to baseball. Both language arts and history are being studied, although your child may not realize it.

You might require him to write a fan letter to his favorite ball teams and pretend that he is the sports writer for your local paper. Can he write as well as the professional? He can at least try. And if you take him in to meet the sports writer, he will try even harder.

He will learn the arithmetic needed to calculate baseball statistics. Use his math textbooks to teach baseball batting averages and ratios. When he can accurately recalculate a player's statistics as they change during a game, he passes math.

He may study the physics of a curve ball in motion. It's simply the centripetal force of the spinning ball, and the atomic mass of the ball overcoming inertia and moving through the gravitational pull of the earth while the friction of the air acts upon the surface of the ball. Almost every major law of the physical universe works together to make a curve ball curve because God loves baseball!

An older child may learn the ugly truth about racial bigotry by studying the history of black players in professional sports. Imagine a time when there were no black players in the major leagues. That is bigotry. When Jackie Robinson stepped onto the field as the first black major-league player, he was a true civil-rights hero.

Though it may be very difficult for a child to understand, he may learn something about our free-market economy by following the labor disputes between the team owners and the baseball players in recent years. (On second thought, forget it. I don't even think I can understand it.)

Elementary school years are part of the lift-off. They comprise the stage that gets your student moving in every area. It is slow going at first, but it picks up speed.

JUNIOR HIGH SCHOOL: This middle school level is the second stage of the rocket launch. It is the pivotal stage. The objective at this point is to achieve a stable orbit from which to give the rocket a final thrust toward its destination. Stability is not a purely academic concern. It is not by accident that this stage corresponds roughly to adolescence. The opposite sex begins to show up on your child's radar. There is no time in a child's life when stability is more important, or more difficult to maintain.

Drawing on our rocket analogy, this is the stage when the family must provide a strong center of gravity. The family, like the earth with its mass, allows the now orbiting adolescent to get into good routines and stable schedules that help him keep his bearings. Adolescents need a strong, stable, family life as a counterbalance to all that is changing in their lives. They become intensely aware of what is going on "out there," and they would like to spend more time with their friends. That is understandable in light of where they are destined to go. But they will not be ready to leave orbit for some time, and so the bonds of gravity at home must be strengthened.

One way to do this is to make your home the center of social life for your child. Increase its gravity by insisting that all friends become "friends of the family" and that your home be a gathering place for friends of all ages. Throw age-integrated parties. Host the church youth group occasionally for a pizza party. Be creative. This allows other young people to walk with the wise (that's you!), and it keeps your young teen from spinning out of orbit and into a peer group. Through it all, your adolescent's studies must not be neglected. He still has a lot to learn.

It is fortunate that just at the time when a young person most needs to find his place in life he can begin the delightful process of sampling all the variety that life has to offer. During this stage you become a *Patron* of your child in the *Arts of Life*. The coach puts on the hat of the patron in the sense of coming alongside the student and supporting his artistic exploration of life itself.

By art, I don't mean mere decoration. As one arty T-shirt puts it, "Great art will not match your couch." The art I mean is any passionate expression of what is important in life. It is a way of saying, "I feel strongly about this." The Bible calls this "zeal."

Effective art *moves* people. It stirs emotions. It can calm, inspire, depress or enrage. That is its purpose. Great art may not find a mass market. No one but another artist or an investor may ever want to buy it. It may not have any real "use." But it succeeds if it is an accurate expression of who the artist was on the day that he created it.

Your adolescent needs to become passionate about something. He needs to have the soul of an artist for at least a little while. Otherwise, he may make a hasty career decision and spend his life doing something he hates, just because he thought it would make good money or because it seemed to be the "responsible" thing to do. My son Josh might still be video taping weddings if he had not thought deeply about who he was and what God wanted him to do.

The goal in junior high is not so much for him to choose a career, as it is for him to get to know the various fields where ideal careers might await him. Remember, this is a pivotal time. You can go anywhere from here. Like an artist, it is time for him to be some-what impractical. When he decides to join a band, don't ask, "What use is this?" That will all come later. Take off your tie. He's being artistic. Help him throw a little paint on the canvas of his life and ask, "Do you like this?" Try lots of things. Taste all thirty-one flavors. Explore many fields.

Picking a field is not the same thing as picking a business or a career. Your child may love sports. But that is a *field*. There are thousands of careers to choose from within that field. Your child may never play a professional game, but he may one day own a business that manufactures baseballs. And he will enjoy every minute of it because it is in a field that he loves. Once he discovers a field that he enjoys, it will guide him to his ultimate destination.

This is where delight-directed study can take wings and fly. A young teen can become a tireless scholar as he explores his various interests. Josh was a gymnast, a cartoonist, an actor, a videographer, etc. If you require that a "scrapbook" be kept as a record of each focus of exploration, his research skills and writing skills will improve along with other basic skills. Volunteer work with various professions work well at this time. Hobbies can be very effective. Business ventures are often a good idea. Set up a lab in the garage. Whatever else you do, invite his best friends to be part of the adventure with him.

Does He Want to Go to College?

This is the time when some very important decisions need to be made. If college is an option you want to keep open, certain subjects will have to be studied just as college preparation. Higher math, science and foreign languages are especially demanding, and it is not easy to make these subjects delightful unless they have some direct relevance to your student's goals. A young scientist will have no problem conquering the most difficult math and science studies. But the young art major who hopes to attend a major school of art may find science and math *boring*. This is where the principle of setting passionate goals becomes so important.

In the process of developing *The Noble Planner*, I became aware of the value of having passionate goals. These are the kinds of goals that make you willing to climb every mountain and swim every sea. No obstacle is too great. Your zeal just keeps you going toward your goal. This is what Paul was talking about when he said, "But one thing I do: Forgetting what is behind and straining toward what is ahead, I press on toward the goal to win the prize for which God has called me heavenward in Christ Jesus" (Phil. 3:13-14).

The writer of Hebrews writes, "Let us fix our eyes on Jesus, the author and perfecter of our faith, who for the joy set before him endured the cross, scorning its shame, and sat down at the right hand of the throne of God." I am not saying that math or science or foreign language studies are as bad as the cross, but for an art student they may come close. The question is, can you endure the pain for the joy of getting into art school? Is your goal passionate enough to carry you through? If not, you may not be able to go the distance. Count the costs of any decision before you do anything else.

By the time many of our students reach collage age, these questions may be moot. College entrance may be very different by then, what with the "information superhighway" and all the new satellite conferencing technology. A credible college education may be available by modem for a very small fee. But for now, these decisions must be made in the junior high years. If a student falls behind in these college entrance subjects, it may effect his or her college options later on. If college is not necessary for the calling your student has in view, then you can enjoy your freedom to prepare for that future without the distractions of unrelated course requirements. But if a profession in medicine or law is in view, make it a passionate goal. Then help him buckle down and do whatever has to be done.

HIGH SCHOOL: As soon as a stable orbit has been achieved in a young person's life, and a sense of direction has developed, it is time for him to graduate into the final thrust stage of high school studies. This is where you become the *Mentor* of your child in the *Business of Life*. At this stage a good student becomes goal oriented. You can toss aside your artist's hat and put on your three-piece suit. It's time to get down to business—family business.

By this I do not mean only career choices, but life choices of all kinds. Marriage lies ahead for most young people. That is the biggest family business decision he will ever make in his life!

How will you help your student through this time? I believe our sons and daughters should avoid the dating scene entirely. It is little more than a training ground for divorce. Some people put more care into hiring a secretary than they do into choosing their life partner. The better route to a lasting marriage is courtship. Young people can get to know one another far better in the context of family life, with parents and siblings discretely nearby. This allows the young couple to see one another in a far more accurate light and keep the relationship from becoming prematurely emotional or physical. My son Josh, though still single and in the midst of his own adventure in this area, has written and spoken extensively on courtship. His ideas are proving to be Biblical, practical and effective.

But courtship is not an alternative to dating for fifteen-year olds. Young people should not court until they are ready to get married. Until then, it is wise to focus on getting ready. The only way that I have seen to keep teenagers out of one another's arms is to give them a bigger, more wonderful goal to offset all the distractions common to their youth. For a young man, that goal should include preparing for a delightful and profitable career, doing something he really enjoys doing. For a young woman, it includes preparing to be the ideal wife, mother and administrative assistant such a passionate, goal-oriented young man will need.

I realize that I may lose a few readers with my "old fashioned" ideas. But in my mind, this takes us back to the doctrine of the goodness of God. I believe the differences between the sexes are there for very good reasons. I also believe that there are wholesome pleasures to be found in accepting the roles our genders bring upon us. Husband and wife, fatherhood and motherhood, are gender-defined roles. Equality before God does not mean interchangeability. A nut and a bolt may be made of exactly the same material, weigh exactly the same and cost the same amount at the hardware store. They are equal. But two bolts or two nuts cannot accomplish what a nut and bolt are designed to do together. They are not interchangeable. It is the same with men and women. There is more than procreation at stake. The difference between masculine and feminine values and perspectives is needed in every area of life. The difference is delightful to both when kept in proper balance.

In the high school years, I believe sons should be prepared intensely and aimed carefully like arrows at specific targets. Psalm 127 tells us so. Daughters are to be equally prepared for all of life, but not *aimed*. Their future husbands will have wonderful targets already in view, and those young men will need the help of our daughters to hit those targets. This is not a matter of putting women down. It is a matter of raising men up.

High school is also the time to toughen up a young man. He should be given hard jobs that stretch his endurance and make him act like a man. Consider it boot camp for godly husbands and fathers. Summer missions can help in this regard. Each young man should be prepared academically, emotionally and spiritually to be some young woman's husband. As Stu Webber has put it, we need to prepare "tender warriors."

Our daughters will need to be strong, but not tough. They should be prepared academically, emotionally and spiritually to be some young man's wife and the joyful mother of his children. There should be no need or desire to wait to have children. Children are a gift from the Lord. If a couple can't afford to have children, odds are they can't afford to be married. Both sons and daughters should receive "marriage education" that includes instruction in the sacred intimacy between a man and his wife.

High school is the time when the issues of adulthood become the proper delight of every young person's life. Rather than waste time in a flurry of teenage social life, most of their energies should be devoted to getting ready to take responsibility. Michael Farris, founder and President of *Home School Legal Defense Association*, once told me that if he had been told he had to pass his bar examination before he could get married, he would have passed it by the time he was twenty. That is the way it should be. The joy of marriage and family and career should add fuel to the rocket. High school and college years should be times of intense focus. It is the final thrust that takes a teen away from his own home and family and to a home and family of his or her own. If we do it right, and our student's delights are strong, our rockets will be headed for the stars.

Practical Pointers

As a home-school teacher, you can decide just how delight-directed you want your program to be. Delight-directed study is not an "all or nothing" proposition. You can start small and move up as your confidence grows and your child's delights begin to glow.

To get started, you can easily energize your child's hobbies. Get behind his sports card collection by going to the next big event for sports card enthusiasts in your area. Start a building project in the backyard. Let him use his skills as best as he is able. Delight-directed summer projects are especially effective ways to draw students into using their basic skills. Building a treehouse or running a lemonade stand may not be new ideas, but they work very well. Not every delightful interest needs to be organized into a formal study. Many are more effective as simple projects.

There is a logical flow to most activities that will draw your student into studying different subjects without the formality of a lesson plan. Josh's experience with his magazine is a good example. The topics of bookkeeping and computer science all related back to the bigger picture of publishing a magazine. Even though you have no formal lesson plan, be sure to document what your student has done. It is still part of your home-schooling program. Keep any literature, take photos, video tape and whatever else is needed to capture the project for future reference.

It is also appropriate to start out with packaged unit studies as an introduction to various unit-study approaches. Published unit studies, when carefully selected and introduced to the student, can be just as delightful as anything you might create on your own. Unit study guides are designed with the general interests of the typical child in view. That is why classic children's books serve as a spring-board for many publishers. Books like *Little House on the Prairie* have a good track record of delighting children. You can easily make use of such material with your child.

As your confidence grows, and you see that your child really is learning what he needs to know, delight-directed studies can take a larger place in your home-school program. This is especially true in the upper elementary grades after basic skills are securely in place. The beams of light passing through a video camera lens in a delight-directed study will be just as much a part of physics as any other beams of light generated in a lab experiment. The question is whether your child understands the physics of light. When your child writes a brochure to promote his business venture, it is just as effective as any writing assignment you might come up with for a literature class. In fact, your student is likely to work and rework his brochure in order to get it right.

When your child is clearly delighted with a topic like horses or computers or sports, the best strategy will be to take the plunge and create a unit-study plan on that particular topic. Use whatever materials are available. It's not difficult. As we saw in the baseball study, you can simply look at each topic under the light of what would normally be separate school subjects. What is the history of the thing, the science related to it, the math, the social studies, the economics, etc? With a Bible in one hand and an encyclopedia set nearby, you can spin a lesson plan very quickly.

Imagine that you and your child are writing and illustrating your own book on the subject of his delight. That is the right idea. With the resources of your local library, you can create entire one-of-a-kind "books" with your child, simply by researching, digesting and reorganizing the material you discover there. Because this process involves so many basic skills (researching, reading, writing, math, etc.) and touches on so many areas of study (history, science, art, etc.), it won't much matter what the topic of study is as long as it delights your student.

You are not left to fend for yourself entirely in this area. Valerie Bendt's excellent books, *How to Create Your Own Unit Studies* and *The Unit Study Idea Book,* are especially helpful. She helps you develop unit-study lesson plans for any topic you wish to explore. You identify the delight, and she will help you organize the lesson plan. She also shows you how to document the learning that takes place in ways that can be compared with the conventional approaches. Her book, *Creating Books With Children,* will guide you through the book-binding process to create finished books out of each study journal. These become family treasures.

Rhonda Robinson's *IHELP Planner* facilitates delight-directed study lesson planning and record keeping in a very effective way. As the mother of eight children, two of which have hearing impairments, her insights are very practical. The more creative you are, the more you will appreciate the flexibility of her lesson planning approach.

However you choose to use it, and whatever materials you decide to use, remember that delight-directed study is the goal for your students. As adults, this approach is the only way they will be able to be the life-long learners God wants them to be. Delight-directed study will teach them how to learn and how to keep up with all changes in their fields of interest. Textbooks must one day make way for reading "real books." Required classes must yield to voluntary study groups. If that is where you want your children to be eventually, why not get them started in that way from the very beginning? They will be delighted.

Summary

In a delight-directed study, a child's interests are fanned to flame and supported in ways that increase his interest in his studies. The child's delight is the spark that ignites everything.

Delight-directed study is based on the doctrine of the *Goodness of God*. Because God is good, every necessary human activity brings with it some kind of wholesome pleasure, and this includes the activity of study.

The use of the word "delight" in God's Word makes it clear that our studies can be delightful, just as food can be delicious. A well-prepared lesson is a feast for the student's mind.

The word "delight" is defined as "a high degree of pleasure or satisfaction of mind. A delight is a more permanent pleasure than joy, and is not dependent on sudden excitement." That means we can count on our child's delights still being there tomorrow. We can build on their delights in our lesson plans.

Delights are more often caught than taught. They are very contagious. We catch them from our closest friends and especially from those we admire. Wise friends will impart wise and wholesome delights. Foolish friends will transmit foolish and harmful delights. For better or worse, we will study whatever it is that delights us.

If we teach our children by our own example how to have good taste and how to maintain the standards of a strong Biblical conscience, we will not have to serve as their gatekeepers forever.

Whatever your delight may be, there is someone out there who has achieved excellence in pursuing it. Christ honors the Queen of

Sheba as an example of one who was willing to travel a long way in order to see for herself the glory of Solomon's kingdom. We can follow her example by seeking out those who are the "Solomons" in our fields of delight.

Impatient attempts to force a student to learn something that holds no interest for him may be like trying to pry open the petals of a rosebud. Good study habits are more likely to be established through pleasant experiences with study, not by threats and punishments.

Teaching a child is like launching a three-stage rocket to the stars. The first stage is lift-off. The second stage is achieving a stable orbit. And the third stage is the final thrust that takes him out of orbit and toward his final destination.

Decisions concerning the study level should not be based on the student's age, but rather on his attitude and ability.

At the elementary school "Lift-Off" stage, you are your child's *Coach* in the *Games of Life*. As a good coach, you will be training him in all the skills and teaching him all the rules he needs in order to play the "games" of reading, writing, arithmetic, spelling, grammar, etc. These games are enjoyable when they are done together with others.

At the junior high "Pivotal Stage" of the rocket launch, the objective is to achieve a stable orbit. Adolescents need a strong family life as their center of gravity. One way to do this is to make your home more of a center of social life for your child. During this stage you become a *Patron* of your child in the *Arts of Life*.

At the High School "Final Thrust" stage of rocket launch, you become the *Mentor* of your child in the *Business of Life*. In the high school years, your sons should be prepared and aimed carefully at specific targets. Daughters should be well prepared, but not aimed.

As a home-school teacher, you can decide just how delight-directed you want your program to be. Delight-directed study is not an "all or nothing" proposition. You can start small and move up as your confidence and your child's delights grow.

I have but a question or two, saith the sage: Who?
What? When? Where? How? and Why? Tell me. Tell me.
Tell me true.

Basil Grant

EIGHT

YES, BUT...

At this point, you may be thinking that home schooling sounds like a good way to fulfill your responsibility for the education of your children, but you have a lot of questions. And you want answers to those questions before you will seriously consider taking your children out of their public or private school. Fine. That's as it should be. And the bottom line is, can home schooling really work in your circumstances?

I think it can, but I understand your concerns. The fact is, I've probably heard each of the questions that are running through your mind any number of times during my workshops all across the country. So let me address the most common questions. Hopefully, I can show you that, indeed, you can be an effective home-schooling parent.

Qualifications

One comment I hear repeatedly is, "I just don't feel qualified. How can I do as well as a trained, certified teacher?"

First, we need to remember that home schooling or tutoring was the normal form of schooling throughout history until just a few decades ago. We're not entertaining new or untested ideas. If parents in ages past could give their children a good education at home, there's no reason to think that *you* can't, especially now that tools, resources, and curricula of the highest quality are readily available everywhere.

Second, we need to keep in mind the fact that God never gives us a responsibility without also providing the means and the strength to fulfill it. He knows our weaknesses and our fears, and He knows we can't do it alone. He's also ready to give us what we need if we'll only ask. Indeed, He wants us to lean on Him and find our sufficiency in Him, rather than to try to do it ourselves. Home schooling, like having children in the first place, will draw you closer to God.

Remember, too, that God is on our side. He wants us to succeed! He wants our homes to be a strong weapon in His hands for the spiritual warfare going on in this world. So if you feel His leading to home school your children, you can be confident of His blessing and help to do it effectively.

Third, we can look at the many more or less average parents who are already home schooling their children and doing a good job of it—parents who often have no more than a high school education themselves, and there are thousands of them. The fact that they're able to make it work means there's a good chance you can, too.

Fourth, just recall for a moment the weak academic record of most public schools. Those schools are staffed almost *entirely* by college-educated, state-certified teachers, and yet they've been frustrated for years in the job of training their students. They often claim it's because parents aren't doing their part. Thus, credentials and training alone can't get the job done. There's no evidence that a certified teacher can do a better job of educating your child than you can. If there were, believe me, we would all hear about it. The NEA is still looking for that evidence.

Finally, there's no one more motivated than *you* to see your child trained well, not only in academics, but in all areas of life, as the Bible mandates. And that motivation to do the job well, to be a good example, and to work at becoming a better teacher, is far more important than a diploma on the wall. If you approach the task with that attitude, you *can* succeed as a teacher for your child. And you will learn as you teach. You'll grow up as a teacher as your children grow up as students.

Time

"I just don't have the time to teach my child. Do you realize how full my schedule is already?" That's another common concern. And it is a legitimate concern. Everybody is very busy.

We've already seen that the best way to teach a child is one-on-one, giving the child undivided attention, carefully monitoring the level of difficulty and the child's progress. Sadly, the typical day-school teacher, with twenty or more students, just can't give any one student much individual attention.

The home-schooling parent, on the other hand, can give a child the personal attention he needs, easily surpassing what the classroom teacher can offer. But that attention is higher in *quality* as well as *quantity*. A far better education can take place in a home in far *less* time than would be necessary in a classroom, because of the quality of the time devoted to instruction in the home. Remember that mother in Nebraska who spent just two hours a day with her daughter and yet advanced her three grade levels in just nine months! That kind of performance is *not* surprising.

Home schooling doesn't *have* to take up all your time—not by any means. It is a matter of quality, not quantity. A shorter, more effective lesson is better for both student and teacher.

Second, certain life-style changes allow more efficient use of the time we have. The ball and chain of "regular school hours" is removed, allowing you to make better use of your daily routine. Mornings and evenings can be used for studies. Afternoons may be free time. Weekends can be school days if you like. Monday can be your child's day off. It's all up to you. In home schooling, you can redesign your schedule to meet your needs, not the professional educator's. Life can be quieter and less hectic.

Third, it's really a matter of priorities. No one can deny that lesson preparation, child discipline, grading, curriculum, shopping, field trips and the other aspects of home schooling, place demands on your time. But even so, we need to ask ourselves these questions: "What other uses could I make of my time that are more important?" And, "what are my family's priorities?" You may discover that all these things work together more smoothly under your management than they ever did when you shared your children with an outside school. If you have real time-management problems, they can be solved by applying the Biblical principles of time management. In my development of *The Noble Planner*, I have outlined these in detail.

I hope that after reading this far, you'll agree that there are few other things you could do that are more worthy of your time and effort. If it's an investment in your children, whatever time it takes to home school is time extremely well spent.

Organization

Another common concern has to do with household organization. "I'm just not well-organized. I could never make it work," I hear some parents say. Well, there is no doubt that you need to be organized to be an effective teacher. But help is available for the disorganized.

For one thing, there are organizers designed specifically for home schooling. My wife, Sono, and I have developed *The Home School Organizer* with the Christian home-schooling families' special needs in view. It has helped many a disorganized teacher chart a course to success. Lesson planning and documentation tools are invaluable to even the most organized household. There are too many details and appointments to keep track of. Important information should not be kept on the backs of envelopes. In an organizer, there is a place for everything. You write it down once, and that is it.

Much help in organization is also provided by the curriculum and other resources you'll use to do the job. A lot of careful thought and research has gone into those materials. Most of them have built-in lesson planning helps, tools, principles, ideas and strategies to make your job easier.

Third, there are many support groups, from the local level to the national, eager to help with organization—and anything else you may need to home school. These are made up of other Christian parents who are home schooling and can share with you the benefits of their experience. The fact is, very few families have to make a go of home schooling all by themselves.

Finally, you can expect to learn right along with your child. Education is a lifetime journey for both pupil and teacher. You don't expect your child to know everything and be able to do every task perfectly before he even starts school; by the same token, you shouldn't expect perfection from yourself, especially not right out of the chute.

So give yourself some room to grow. Be reasonable in your expectations. There's no reason your organizational ability can't improve over time, along with your other teaching skills.

The Daily Grind

"I don't think I could handle it day in and day out," some parents say. "What about me? When will I ever get away? How will I ever get relief from the kids?" Not every mother may say this out loud, but most have thought it. These are understandable concerns. After all, you spend quite a bit of time with your child every day, anyway. Sending him to school five days a week can provide something of a welcome break for both of you. It's also true that teaching every day can become a grind, like any other job, no matter how much you love your child.

But my experience has been that parents who think they can't handle that much time with their kids are those who also think they shouldn't take charge of the child's schedule. Because they only see the child in a "vacation" or "after school" context, they feel they can't set the pace and give an assignment. In home schooling, you are authorized to give direction. Because of that, the child is not as bored as he might be during summer breaks.

Speaking of summer breaks, you might be better off not even having one. Many home schools, my own included, operate year-round with a two-week break every ten to twelve weeks, just like colleges. This eliminates the long summer vacation and the "academic amnesia" that usually results. You will be able to travel as a family any time of the year, and the rhythm of the year will be much more pleasant.

The advantage of flexibility that home schooling has over the classroom situation definitely works in your favor. If, on a given day, the school routine just isn't working for you or your child, or if you just need a break, you can take a day off. Since you set your own schedule, you have the freedom to do that. You don't have to feel locked into it on a day when things aren't going well.

Now, you obviously can't afford to take a day off too many times in a year, and you don't want to make a habit (which your child would pick up) of walking away from tough situations in life. But neither should you ignore those times when a break is necessary for both your sakes.

And, finally, don't let home schooling (or parenting, for that matter) totally dominate your life. You are more than a mommy or daddy. You need to maintain social contacts with friends and be involved in outside activities you enjoy. You need to have regular "dates" with your spouse—just the two of you. There is a time to come apart for a while before you fall apart forever.

If you can keep that kind of balance in your life so that the relationship with your child doesn't become your whole existence, you'll be less likely to find the home-schooling experience a grind. A Mother's Day Out can be arranged by having a Grandmother's Day In. If Grandma can't or won't watch the children for an occasional afternoon, adopt a grandma from your church. You might also hire a maid to do about three hours of cleaning every week or two. These are good investments of time and money. Note to husbands: encouraging your wife to get out once in a while is just good management. Don't let her burn out.

Socialization

"Our child needs the social contact with other kids," many parents say. "How do we provide that if we home school?"

As we've already mentioned, there are really only two kinds of socialization: age-integrated and age-segregated. Unfortunately, what usually goes on in day schools is age-segregated socialization; a child is pressured to adopt the habits and attitudes of peers, while his identity in reference to home and church is frequently attacked. Steady contact with parents and older and younger siblings provided by home schooling, on the other hand, offers age-integrated socialization, resulting in children who know how to relate to and get along with people of all ages.

The Biblical solution to providing social training for children is practicing hospitality. When families invite other families over for an evening or allow them to stay overnight in their guest room or in children's vacated bedrooms, everyone develops a depth of friendship that will last a lifetime. International friendships, established by entertaining foreign students and missionaries, later bloom into opportunities for international travel. Home-schooled children have more, not less, contact with others if their parents practice hospitality.

Children enjoy having contact with a few age-mates, however. This is necessary in order for them to develop personal friendships. Such wholesome friendships can be rewarding if given wise counsel and parental supervision. But kids don't normally find that in a classroom setting. It is when they participate in projects and service events with a few other children that friendship develops. Extracurricular activities such as sports clubs, scouting, choir, and so on, can afford wholesome friendships. My son Joshua's gymnastics team was a valuable social experience for him, but it had its drawbacks. It introduced music, language and styles of dress of which we did not approve. It is never wise to leave a group of children alone for long periods of time to pool their inexperience. Better to allow children to become friends of your entire family.

Further social contact comes from church activities, get-togethers with family and friends and joint activities, such as field trips with support groups. When you stop and think of all the opportunities available for social contact and growth with peers, you realize a classroom experience isn't necessary at all.

Isolation

"Isn't home schooling really just a way to run away from the world? I want my child to be able to survive in the real world and help change it for the better." This is another legitimate concern; we and our children can't be salt and light in the world if we're not *in* it in the first place.

The questions I would raise in response are, how do you prepare children to deal with the "real" world, and at what point do you ask them to stand up for Christ in it? Perhaps a few analogies can help us find the answers.

First, imagine taking a newborn foal that's just learning to run and asking it to compete against the mature, thoroughly trained three-year-old horses in the Kentucky Derby. That wouldn't make much sense, would it? It's obvious to anyone that the foal wouldn't stand a chance. Yet, there are many people who think nothing of throwing a five or six-year-old child into an educational system designed by intelligent, well-trained adults to instill anti-Christian, anti-family values. When should a young horse enter the races?

Hopefully, not until after he has been trained and has won a few time trials on the family farm. Premature competition will cause the young foal to become permanently fearful of the race.

Or picture a tomato seedling. You plant it in your greenhouse in hopes that it will become strong and healthy. You know it is better to start the plant in a protected place where it can develop roots and maturity in safety and warmth. It would be foolish to set it out prematurely in the harsh elements, subject to cold and wind. Of course, you don't want bland and pithy "greenhouse tomatoes"; this vine will one day bear its fruit in the field. You are simply preparing the seedling for transplantation at the *appropriate* time. In the same way, a child will be much better prepared to make his way in the world and stand firm in his faith if he's had a chance to develop in the protected environment of home and church. How long does that take? You know your child. Jesus made a point of warning us not to make little ones sin.

This doesn't mean you will hide your child entirely from the world. We don't want to raise children to be naive. But it does mean we control when and where and how they learn about this world. We do that best by including them in our own ministry to the world. When we practice hospitality, we deal with the world outside our home from a position of strength and authority. We need not allow happenstance to choose the lessons our children learn. We act as the gatekeepers of our children's experiences, regulating their access to the world and the world's access to them. By being with them most of the time, we can help them understand what's happening around them, as well as teach them how they can respond from a Christian perspective. Our goal is insolation, not isolation.

Home schooling, then, isn't an attempt to run from the world, but a simple, realistic strategy of how best to train a child to deal with that world at the appropriate time. And that appropriate time is after the child has proved his maturity and Christian character at home.

Legal Complications

The possibility of legal problems should be a concern for anyone who is considering home schooling. Most of us have heard of parents who were taken to court by a local school board for their insistence on home schooling. Understandably, no one relishes such a prospect for himself, and it's made us wonder: is home schooling legal?

Home schooling is, indeed, legal. Hundreds of thousands of children all over the country, from kindergarten through high school, are being home schooled without legal problems. According to the Home School Legal Defense Association in Washington, D.C., laws permitting the practice are now on the books in forty-two of the fifty-five United States' jurisdictions (the fifty states plus American Samoa, the District of Columbia, Guam, Puerto Rico and the Virgin Islands). And those states in which it's not already explicitly permitted by law are currently considering the issue.

It should be said, too, that while the states don't have the right to prohibit home schooling, they do attempt to regulate it as they would like to regulate all private schools. Some of the regulations are not onerous, but are meant to ensure the health and safety of children. Other regulations are for the legal protection of the state itself. Look at these regulations carefully, but don't automatically assume that they're designed to frustrate your desire to educate your own child. Government officials are honestly worried that your child will grow up and sue them for not making certain he got a good education.

All that notwithstanding, no one can guarantee that you can home school without fear of trouble. The laws aren't uniform from state to state, and even in a state that has a good law on the books, a state or local official antagonistic to home schooling can create a problem. We should also remember that, since home schools are very effective in training up children who are weapons for God in spiritual warfare, Satan is strongly opposed to them. The devil will try to intimidate and stop us whenever and wherever he can. While we're on the subject, the National Education Association is also on record against home schooling; like most labor unions, they prefer a "closed shop" with no outside competition.

The chances are good that you'll be able to home school without any trouble, but as part of your research in preparation for the possibility of home schooling, you'll need to check into the situation in your area. Talk with other home-schooling families and write to the Home School Legal Defense Association (see appendix). They will know what is going on in your state. The law is certainly not something you should ignore or take lightly.

Remember that, regardless of what your state laws may say, the Constitution of the United States is on your side, especially in the First, Ninth, and Fourteenth Amendments. There is also a growing number of lawyers throughout the nation who are prepared to help home-schooling parents when legal problems do arise.[1] Remember, too, that God is with you in this adventure. Once you've done your homework, there is no need to fear the legal complications.

Summary

Don't be afraid to ask questions. But don't allow those questions to be a stumbling block that will keep you from doing what you know is right, either.

Remember, home schooling is no novelty. It was the norm until very recently, and, besides, God has given you this responsibility. Where God guides, He provides.

You are qualified: they are your children. You do have the time: you have all the time you need to fulfill your obligations. You can develop your organizational skills. You can deal with every objection and concern. The only unanswered question that remains is: Are you prepared to trust God to be with you as you take this step of faith?

It is a terrifying thing to begin. To begin anything at all. The rewards are but rumors then. The glories are but gossip. To taste and see, we must venture into the murky waters of inexperience. And that is, indeed, a terrifying thing. But 'tis more terrifying still to stand ashore and only wish it could someday truly be true.

Tristam Gylberd

FIRST THINGS FIRST

A man was once seen wandering through a remote area of the Midwest, looking confused. One of the locals asked him if he needed any help. "No thanks," he said. "I'm doing fine."

"Well, where is it you're going?" the local asked. "Maybe I can give you some directions at least."

"I don't know what I'm looking for," the man answered with a smile, "but I'll recognize it when I see it!"

The man's search was the epitome of the old saying, "Aim at nothing and you'll hit it every time." That kind of approach to anything in life—especially in something as important as education—simply won't get the job done. It's just asking for frustration and failure. To reach our goals, we need to know where we're going and how to get there. We need a plan, and we need to know how to get started. Unfortunately, most parents wander through the educational woods as aimlessly as that man wandered through the Midwest. This needs to change.

Counting the Cost

The first step in getting started is to count the cost. Common sense and Scriptural wisdom tell us that, before we start anything, we had better know all the costs involved and be sure we're both willing and able to pay them. It's a foolish person who starts something and then discovers halfway through that he can't, or won't, pay the price to finish (Luke 14:28).

There are costs to home schooling, and we need to face that right from the beginning. You'll hear it said that home schooling takes less time than conventional schooling, and it's true, but not less of your time. It takes less of your child's time. He gets more done faster. Home schooling takes less energy, too. But not less of your energy. Your child will make more progress without getting worn out. It is also suggested that home schooling takes less money than a private school. That may be true, but only because you are willing to work cheap. If you ever start charging what your services are worth, it will be too expensive to continue.

So home schooling, while it is still a good value, costs time and effort. And it will require you to spend some of your money. In fact, there's a substantial outlay needed in the beginning. Don't make the mistake of thinking that home schooling is a cheap way to educate. If you want cheap, the public schools are the cheap way to go. You have less out-of-pocket costs. Home schooling, properly executed, will cost you about $100 to $200 per student per year. Call around to see what private schools charge, and you will have a fair estimate of what you will be saving in your home school for the first year. But you still have to invest.

You might think that you can do it more cheaply. You'll cut corners. Well, that's just not the right approach. You don't have to be extravagant, but your child's education isn't a place to skimp. Save on clothes. Save on vacations. But don't try to save on your child's education. If you do, it will cost you more in the long run if you try.

If you're going to home school, part of your preparation and planning should be figuring out just what it will cost and just how you'll afford it. This might mean having a garage sale, starting a family business venture or delaying the replacement of an old but adequate car. But figure it out and establish a reasonable budget before you move ahead.

Keep in mind that the initial expense is a renewable investment. Once you are through with textbooks and other supplies for one year, you can usually sell them and recoup a substantial part of your initial expenditure. Many support groups now host an annual curriculum fair which serves as a swap meet for home-schooling families with used curricula. Make your children take good care of their books.

Making the Commitment

Once you've counted the costs, think it all through, talk it over with your spouse at length, and pray through the various decisions together. Don't rush the decision-making process. Take the time you need so that both of you will be in agreement and at peace with what you're going to do.

Once you've decided to home school, be resolute. Don't doubt in the darker moments what God has shown you in the light. The time, effort and expense of preparation, coupled with the adjustment your child will have to make if he's already been in school, dictate that it not be a decision lightly made or entered into tentatively. There may be some resistance. Don't enter it thinking you'll just bail out quickly if it doesn't go as well as you had hoped. It probably won't, at first. Make a commitment that you'll do whatever it takes to succeed for at least one year. Families that make it through the first year usually continue for many more years. Also, resist the temptation to let your child decide. If he or she has friends in school, the decision will be predictable. Make a decision you believe your child will thank you for when he is thirty years old.

Setting a Realistic Time Frame

Once you have counted the cost and made your commitment, allow yourself a realistic time frame in which to get started. You will need a preparation period of thirty days at least. During that time, you'll have a lot of things to do to get ready, a lot of decisions to make; these things shouldn't be done hastily. "Decide in haste, regret at leisure," as the old cliche says.

I realize you may be watching your child come home from school with all the signs of peer-dependency and, perhaps, a poor attitude toward studying. It is easy to feel justified in just jerking him out in one day. But then you take the risk of being scrutinized by the authorities before you have had time to set up the home-school program. You'll look a little truant if all you can say is, "The books are in the mail."

If you're diligent in your preparation, you can probably do most of what's needed in about thirty days. However, if you're ordering anything through the mail, as many home-schooling parents do, you will need to allow more time or borrow materials temporarily from another family. Don't begin empty-handed.

And having made a commitment in such an important area as your child's education, don't hurt your chances for success by rushing through the all-important preparation stage too quickly.

Enlisting Support

Once you've counted the cost and made the commitment, the next step in really getting started is enlisting support from a variety of sources. First, join and participate in local and state Christian home-school associations. Here you'll find experienced Christian parents to help you, other beginners to commiserate with and a group of people with whom you and your child can do fun things, such as gather for park days, gym days, skating parties and field trips. You can also pool talents and resources to provide things that individual parents can't do easily—like co-op classes for science labs, oil painting, and band. Co-ops inject a great deal of creativity and innovation into your home-school adventure.

As you get involved in these support groups, you'll no doubt find one or two other parents with whom you get along best and whose counsel you can seek when you have questions or concerns. Ideally, one of these people will be someone with more experience in home schooling than you. But even if not, two heads and hearts are better than one.

An excellent source of teaching support comes from the various home-schooling magazines. The tips, news, and sharing of experience you'll find there are well worth the subscription price. These magazines are full of resources for Christian home-schooling families.

Choosing Your Tools

One of the biggest steps in getting started, of course, is choosing the tools you'll use to teach. By that I mean the curricula out of which the majority of your teaching will come. I will address this step in depth in the next chapter, but for now it is good to remember Marva Collins' classic statement, "Anything works if the teacher works." In other words, it is your diligence in the long run that makes your teaching a success, not the curriculum. A well-organized curriculum is like a good cook book. It tells you what to do, and it provides you with most of the ingredients. But in the art of teaching, you are still the "cook." You must adapt the recipe to make it a great educational meal.

I know many a great home-schooling mother who thinks she has found the perfect curriculum for phonics or math. When I ask, "What else have you tried?" she answers, "Nothing. Why should I, when this one is working so well?" She doesn't realize that she is giving all the credit to the curriculum when, in fact, she is just working faithfully under God's blessing with what may be an average program.

For specific and up-to-date guides to curriculum, I invite you to write to me at Christian Life Workshops for our current issue of Home School Favorites. We offer special prices on all the most useful resources and curricula. Our catalog will help you make your curriculum choices, grade by grade, in every subject of study.

When you begin, you will probably be unsure about the study level that is appropriate for your child. You have several options for placement tests and diagnostic tests. Several curriculum publishers offer these services by mail. Also, local Christian schools may be willing to administer the placement tests they normally use. It is unwise to assume that your child is at his grade level in any given subject. He may be far ahead or far behind.

You'll also need a good study Bible, an exhaustive Bible concordance, a good Bible dictionary, and a newer set of encyclopedias. These are standard equipment in any Christian home school.

Another tool you'll want to use is *The Encyclopedia of Truths for School Subjects* by Dr. Ruth Haycock. Developed originally for the Christian schools, this volume takes thirty subjects of school study and draws out of the Bible everything it has to say about them. It summarizes each concept, provides the Biblical background, and prints the actual passages of Scripture, or a synopsis of a longer passage, under each heading. This volume allows home-schooling parents to easily consult the Bible on any topic of study. If you want your children to study in the light of God's Word, this is one of your best investments.

Optional, but useful, are legal, medical and household maintenance manuals. Keep your eyes open for chalk and bulletin boards, a desk, chairs, lighting, maps, a globe, writing and art supplies, tape recorder and record player, flip chart and easel. All these things tend to come to those who wait—and go to garage sales. You won't need all these things immediately, but you will want them eventually. Keep a mental list and keep your eyes open for good buys. No doubt other books you read and other parents you talk to will bring other tools to your attention as well.

Organizing, Facilitating, and Planning

There's no substitute for good planning and organization. For example, you'll need to plan how to use the space in your home most efficiently for schooling. It's good to teach the same subjects in the same places each day; this practice establishes a routine which encourages concentration and studiousness. The dining room table is often a place for things like Math and English, the kitchen table is a good place for crafts, and so on. (Teach your child that it's okay to make a mess, but not okay to leave one.)

You may need to install some bookshelves in a convenient place and clear some storage space. Since most of us are pack rats, you may need to call the Salvation Army or hold a garage sale so you'll have adequate storage for school supplies.

Planning well means setting aside at least a half hour per week to think ahead and prepare upcoming lessons and activities. In *The Noble Planner*, I suggest making this planning time a Sunday afternoon routine. Planning in the afterglow of worship is the best planning of all. Field trips, for example, need to be planned to coincide with major subjects of study. Your child should also study ahead of the trip to be prepared for it, and there should be follow-up activities afterward to get the maximum benefit from the excursion. The *Yellow Pages Guide to Educational Field Trips* will help you do this.

With your child's textbooks, you may wish to determine before the beginning of the year how many pages per week you'll need to cover in order to stay on schedule and finish the books by the end of the term. In this way, from week to week, you'll know if you're ahead of schedule or falling behind. Then you can make necessary adjustments before you get too far off track.

The issue of getting ahead or falling behind brings up the question of whose schedule to follow, the textbook's or the child's? Some children need more time to grasp a concept. What will you do when you are falling behind?

When I was a teenager, I used to get work on nearby farms cleaning stalls. In the Midwest, work was always piling up somewhere. On one occasion, I was in a big hurry, and instead of cleaning the stall as I should, I was just grooming it a little. I was knocking off the high places and filling in the low places to make it look better. To my surprise, the farmer was watching my ruse.

"Gregg," he asked, "You in a hurry?"

"Yes, I guess I am," I admitted.

"Well, if you don't have time to do it right, you sure don't have time to do it over."

His advice has come back to me many times when I am under pressure to meet a deadline. If I don't have time to do it right, do I have time to go back and do it all over? In home schooling, sometimes a student needs more time than the textbook publisher thought was necessary. Do you hurry up and finish on time, only to go back and repeat the entire grade in that subject? No. Take the time you need to do it right. So what if you take a year and a half to finish second-grade arithmetic? Take a year and a half. But please don't make your child go back to do it over, just because you wanted to go faster than he could handle. Don't dawdle. But don't hurry, either.

If you are an inexperienced teacher with no Sunday school experience or other teaching background, pick up a few short books on how to teach. Ruth Beechick's book, *You Can Teach Your Child Successfully*, is excellent. But most of the methods you'll need will be built right into the curriculum you are using. The teacher's manual can be very helpful. Your contacts with other home-schooling parents and your own growing experience will help you learn and grow as a teacher.

Exercising Discipline

As soon as you really get rolling in your new home-school venture, you'll likely run into the toughest problem of all: exercising and maintaining proper discipline. Discipline in the home-schooling situation is a major concern of many parents. And rightly so. "Will my child respect me and work for me as he would his teacher?" people often ask. "Wouldn't it be easier for someone else, an objective outsider, to handle him?"

There's no doubt that some children work better for a stranger than they do for their own parents. But even then, it isn't right. And it can change. Success depends on whether your child respects you as his parent; whether you've previously been successful in building discipline into the relationship and into your child's life.

You see, when you home school, your new relationship to your child as teacher can't be separated from your relationship as his mom or dad. If you haven't taught your child to respect and obey you before you begin to home school, you can't expect some miraculous transformation in the relationship to take place on the first day of study.

On the other hand, if you have a basically good, respectful relationship with your child, you can, in fact, teach your child more effectively than anyone else. The real-life experiences of thousands of home-schooling parents have demonstrated this over and over again. Most parents can be very effective teaching their own children.

The proper exercise of parental discipline is a subject deserving full and careful treatment—treatment that's outside the scope of this book. But for our purposes, there are a few basic points that should be made here.

First, as darling and lovable as kids are, and as much as they are a gift from God, the fact remains that they're all born with a sinful nature. Draw a line, and they will step across it. If that nature is left unchecked, children soon become unruly and rebellious. Later, they become adults who lack self-control. They inflict great harm on themselves and others. And they have great difficulty bowing their hearts to God to be saved.

We must never allow romanticism about the noble savage, unrestrained by civilization, or the modern liberal notion of the perfectibility of man (which is, actually, neither modern nor liberal—it is ancient and heretical) to distort our understanding of that reality. Children need discipline. In fact, children want discipline. They want help in doing what they know is right.

The sinfulness of children is the reason that discipline must include, not only training in and rewarding of right behavior, but also the instilling of a hatred of wrong behavior and a healthy fear of its consequences. That is what discipline provides.

Second, for discipline to be loving and effective, it must be consistent. Children need to know what the rules are and that those rules don't change from minute to minute. They may test those rules and even rebel against them, but clearly-defined rules actually provide a boundary of security around a child. He finds comfort in knowing that his parents are in charge. If he knows exactly how to get a spanking, he also knows how to avoid that spanking.

The key to child training seems to be consistency. I've seen many different styles of discipline bear good fruit because they were applied consistently over many years. Doubting and wavering in the child's presence is a sure invitation for a confrontation. If wrong behavior or attitudes by the child are supposed to result in certain disciplinary actions every time, take those actions every time. Don't wait until you feel angry enough to discipline. Discipline without anger. Otherwise, children will learn quickly that Mom and Dad's words can be ignored, that Mom and Dad don't back up what they say, that the rules can be broken. And once kids learn that, discipline is out the window. For a list of resources to help you establish proper discipline, see the back pages.

Legal Considerations

Given the constant flux in the legal status of home schooling, part of getting started must include obtaining the most up-to-date information on laws and court challenges in progress in your state. Begin your search with the local home-school association, which should have what you need. If, by some chance, the people there don't have the information, they can surely tell you where to find it.

When you get this information, realize that what you see is just a snapshot of the law in progress. Remember those cute pictures you took of your child when he was first born? How long did he contin-ue to look like that? Not very long. In the same way, the picture you get of the legal situation will tell you what it's like today, but under-stand that it's subject to sudden change. Keep abreast of what's hap-pening in your state. A single court case can change everything.

Once you know the current status of the law in your state, you can determine the best way to set up your home school. In some states, for example, it's best to file as a private school. In others, you file an affidavit. Here again, your local or state home-school associa-tion should be able to advise you.

No matter what the laws may be, apply for membership with the Home School Legal Defense Association. That way, in case you are challenged by local authorities, your legal fees will be covered by the national defense fund. This organization will ask you to fill out some forms to explain, among other things, your reasons for wanti-ng to home school. Don't panic. Their purpose in asking questions is to establish in their own minds that they would have grounds on which to defend you in court, should it prove necessary to do so. They know what you will probably say. But they want to have you say it in your own words, with your own references to Scripture.

Keep in mind that the Home School Legal Defense Association will not accept you into membership if you are already involved in a legal complication. You cannot buy car insurance for a wreck you have already had. Neither should you expect to be insured for a legal battle already in progress. Join the association before you are contacted by school authorities.

Once you're accepted for membership, the Association will defend you free of charge if you're ever charged with a violation of law for home schooling your child. And even if you never need their defense, by joining you stand with home-schooling parents everywhere in fighting for your constitutional and parental rights.

Annual dues for membership in the Association are a bargain. When you consider that a legal conflict at even the lowest court level can cost you three thousand dollars or more in attorney's fees, the dues are a good and reasonable insurance investment. "Don't stay home without it."

As you prepare to home school, be careful to file, in a timely fashion, any necessary affidavits or letters of intent with the appropriate authorities. Otherwise, your child could be considered truant. However, do not ask for permission to home school unless you are willing to comply if the authorities say, "No." Grant voluntary and reasonable information to the authorities, but explain that in doing so you are not acknowledging their authority to grant or deny permission for you to obey God's commandments. Mention your religious convictions from the very beginning.

When you deal with any school or governmental authorities regarding your child's schooling, always approach them with a positive, respectful attitude. You do this in part because you're a disciple of Christ, obeying God's command to honor all those in authority. People are also more friendly and cooperative, when you are. Be sure, too, to get any agreements and understandings in writing, because the people with whom you deal may have faulty memories or may leave their jobs and be replaced by others unfamiliar with, or even unsympathetic to, your cause. The best memory is never as useful in court as the most faded ink on paper.

Records and Documentation

For your own sake and for the sake of your children, it's imperative that you keep complete, accurate and up-to-date records on each of your students. These records demonstrate that you are, in fact, teaching, and that your child is making reasonable academic progress.

The records you keep should include the following: attendance, grades in each subject, lesson plans by subject and health records (height, weight, vision and auditory tests, immunizations and diseases).

Make sure that these records are neat, comprehensive, and professional. They may prove to be your best ally if ever local authorities begin to question the legitimacy of your school. *The Home School Organizer*, mentioned earlier, provides all the forms needed for this purpose in an integrated, reproducible format. It will save you time and expense if you will use it consistently.

Starting Slowly

Finally, as you're getting started, take it easy on yourself. Don't try every creative teaching method you've ever read about in the first week. Get your feet wet first and gain some confidence. Develop your skills as you go along; you're learning right alongside your child.

Gradually, as your skills develop and your confidence increases, you can do more and teach more creatively. But all in good time. Don't set yourself up for an early disappointment that will ruin your enthusiasm. And, remember, the national average in the public schools is not that hard to beat. Do your best, that's all.

Summary

Have a plan.

Count the cost. Realize before you begin that, like anything else worthwhile, home schooling your children will cost time, effort, and money. It's an investment in your children.

Make the commitment. Both you and your spouse should be of one mind. Commit to stick it out for at least one year.

Be prepared. Allow thirty days to gather materials for review and to order your curricula by mail.

Enlist support. Join local and state Christian home-school associations for information on support groups, co-op classes and counsel.

Gather your tools. A carpenter wouldn't think of going to work without his tools. Neither should you.

Get organized. Establish a routine—teach subjects in the same place daily. Maximize your resources.

Exercise discipline. Home schooling doesn't begin in a vacuum. If your child respects you, teaching and learning will be easier. If he's hard to discipline, don't expect miracles. Buckle down, set some limits on his behavior and be consistent.

Legal considerations. Keep abreast of the laws pertaining to home schooling in your state. Join the Home School Legal Defense Association.

Keep clear records and documentation. Keep complete records on academic progress, attendance, lesson plans and health records.

Start slowly. Wade slowly into your pool of teaching methods. You'll gain confidence and creativity in time.

Getting started should be a genuinely enjoyable experience. And the adventure will have just begun.

The object of education is to prepare the young to educate themselves throughout their lives.

Robert Maynard Hutchins

TEN

HOW TO SELECT A CURRICULUM

Dr. Paul Vitz asserts

I assume the reader already acknowledges that the content of
school textbooks is important. The facts, interpretations, and
values taught to today's children will largely determine the
character of tomorrow's citizenry. Indeed, it has been said that
to control the content of a nation's textbooks is to control
that nation's future.[1]

Clearly, there is a lot more to education than just the books that
are used. Probably the most influential teaching we do is through
our example. Nonetheless, we should not underestimate the importance of the curricula we use. Choosing the material that fits our
family's lifestyle is one of our primary tasks as home schoolers.

Principles for Choosing a Curriculum

There are many home-school curricula to choose from—so
many, in fact, that it's impossible to keep up with them all. New
products are introduced every few months. Probably the most
important step in choosing a curriculum, then, is to ask experienced
home schoolers what has been working well for them. Naturally,
you'll want to concentrate on people who have done a good job of
teaching their own children and whose opinions you trust.

When you discuss curriculum, ask about the pros and cons of
the curricula they've used. Ask what they liked best and least about
them. As part of your assessment of the best curriculum for you and

your child, you will need to compare the basic types of programs which are available. There are three main types: (1) the more traditional textbooks that feature the kind of teacher-student interaction which we're all familiar with from the conventional classroom; (2) self-directed study materials that emphasize the more or less independent use of workbooks and other programmed learning materials; and (3) delight-directed study materials that emphasize unit studies, study projects, and learning-by-doing activities, which allow the student greater freedom under the direction of a teacher.

The question of which material is best cannot be answered any better than the question of which flavor of ice cream is best. Preferences differ, philosophies differ and, to be honest, teaching circumstances differ.

A family with two or three students may find the traditional textbook approach works best. The content is in the text, and a teacher's manual and study questions at the end of each chapter guide in discussion and learning activities. This is by far the most popular approach, partly because it is most familiar to the parents who are doing the teaching.

Another family with four to fourteen students may find that the self-directed, programmed materials are best. These materials place less demand on the teacher. That doesn't mean the students are left to fend for themselves. The programmed materials can be taught just like a regular textbook. They just don't have to be taught in every case, because they are designed to be studied independently. There is no denying that these materials can get the job done if the teaching parent uses them as they were designed to be used.

A third family may choose unit study materials. These materials attempt to integrate the usual subjects of study into a learning project or activity. Some unit studies are built on Biblical character traits. Others use a passage of Scripture as a foundation and then explore the various tangents suggested by words in the passage. Jesus said that those who hear His word and obey Him are like those who build a house on the rock; the storms cannot make it fall. In such a passage we might study the inner ear, architecture, geology and weather. Over a period of time, children involved in such studies gain a broad grasp of their world and the Bible, which illuminates it.

Some of the best unit study materials are organized around classic children's literature. These seem to hold the child's interest better than other approaches, while still incorporating Biblical and character training. In the early grades, you will still have to supplement for phonics and basic math.

Selecting Your Curricula

There are several good books that review individual home-school curricula, and I would encourage you to study these. Cathy Duffy's *Home Educators' Curriculum Manuals* are indispensable in evaluating home-school material. These are for elementary school and junior and senior high school. Mrs. Duffy tells you in no uncertain terms what she thinks of the material available at each grade level. She's very specific and holds strong, very helpful opinions. She's also one of the pioneers in the home-school movement, as curriculum specialist for the Christian Home Education Association of California. Based on the proven results of her counsel to thousands of Christian families, you'd have to agree that she knows what she's talking about. (See Home School Resources)

Once you start reading these books and talking to your local contacts, you'll probably find that several names are being mentioned more often than others. Choose those curricula to review first, and do so most carefully.

When you have a list of two or three curricula that you think are worth further investigation, if time allows, make arrangements to borrow those materials from a local family that is using them. Your local support group may hold a meeting where everyone brings their curriculum for others to look over. Ask if this will be arranged in time for you to make your decisions. As a last resort, you may need to order the materials you are interested in and look them over. Many suppliers offer an examination period in which you may return products for a refund. Once you have the curriculum in hand, evaluate each in light of the following questions:

- First, (if it is from a Christian publisher) does it glorify Christ clearly throughout? If not, does it offend your Christian faith?

- Second, is it well-organized for both the teacher and the child?

- Third, is it flexible, allowing you to adapt it to your child's needs?

- Fourth, are humanism and evolution presented in relation to ethics and origins?

- Fifth, does the material allow for a lot of student-teacher interaction without requiring a teacher's constant involvement? You want to teach, but you also want your child to be able to study independently at times.

- Sixth, does the curriculum throw in too much busy work for classroom use? You can always skip over excessive practice problems in math, but why pay for something you won't use in a home-school setting?

- Seventh, does the publisher provide a teacher's manual? In some cases you can teach right from this manual without having to buy a student text. Teachers' manuals give suggestions for approaching a topic successfully.

- Eighth, is it eye-appealing? Does your child respond well to it?

Naturally, each curriculum reflects a certain religious bias, whether it be Evangelical, Fundamentalist, Catholic or something else. You'll want to pick one consistent with your own beliefs and the values you want to pass on to your child. The curriculum manuals will help you sort through this aspect of the many choices available.

Once you've made your choice, if you are using textbooks, I suggest you use one publisher's complete line for at least the first year, until you're more experienced. We tend to try to become gourmet cooks, so to speak, when we still haven't learned to fry an egg. So, we tend to go for one curriculum that's best in math, another that's best in history, a third that's best in science, and so on.

The problem with this approach is that most major curricula are integrated, making them difficult to mix and match. A publisher may assume that students are already familiar with each of the texts in a particular grade. If you're mixing and matching, you won't have that familiarity, and many of your lessons may seem to lack vital information. If you are using unit study materials, this will not be a problem because the entire program is integrated.

As you become more experienced and confident as a teacher, however, you can do some mixing and matching and adjusting of existing material to suit you and your children's needs best. Indeed, there's a lot of room for creativity in teaching, once you know what you're doing.

Because of delays in the mail and other hazards, be sure to order your curriculum as early as possible so that you will have plenty of time to become thoroughly familiar with it and prepared to teach it before the beginning of your school term.

Summary

Although the most influential teaching you do is by the example you set, choosing a good curriculum takes an extremely high priority.

The problem is that you'll find so many to choose from. Remember, talk to some home-schooling veterans. Ask them what has worked and what hasn't; what they liked best and least. Don't try to go it alone. Let Mary Pride, Cathy Duffy, and CLW be your counselors. Read the books.

Browse for a while before you buy. Shop smart.

If you're going to go to all the trouble of home schooling in the first place, it is only reasonable that you will take the utmost care in selecting the tools that will help you do that job right.

Education is the transmission of civilization.
It is the laboratory of life.

Will and Ariel Durant

LABORATORY OF LIFE

How do people come to know Christ? They come to know Him in the laboratory of Christian family life. According to research conducted by a wide variety of demographic and church growth experts, new Christians fall into about eight basic categories:

- Four to six percent are converted as church walk-ins
- Four to seven percent are drawn by the pastor's reputation
- Two to four percent come in through special programs
- Only .01 percent respond to city-wide crusades
- Two to four percent have special needs met
- One to two percent respond to visitation ministries
- Four to six percent receive Christ in Sunday school
- *The remaining seventy-eighty percent are won by friends and relatives.*

Those figures indicate that the Gospel is best spread through the relationships people already have. Evangelism is the work of the whole Church, not just pastors or evangelists. It is especially the work of families. It is a function of life's grand laboratory: the home.

How can your home be used to play an exciting part in God's work? How can you train your children to lead dynamic and evangelistic Christian lives?

The answer is by practicing hospitality.

Wherever your children go in life, they'll need the skills that come from first-hand experience in dealing with different kinds of people and different age groups. Practicing hospitality helps children develop those important social skills. And it opens a whole new field of dynamic evangelism for them and for us.

For our children to learn hospitality, we need to set goals and develop a strategy, just as in any other kind of education. We can't simply invite people with children to our homes for a meal and say to our kids, "Socialize with one another. Learn to get along." If we do, we end up with pooled ignorance and immaturity, peer dependency and intimidation.

Part of the training we give our kids, then, is how to be a good host or hostess—how to make a guest feel comfortable, how to meet a guest's needs and entertain him, how to be courteous and have proper manners. We can coach them in these areas and have them learn from our example.

A home is a natural place for a child to learn these things because it's a place of great security. Because it's *his* home, the child enjoys territorial authority and, therefore, an additional sense of confidence.

Since my wife and I have taught our children some of these skills, when a family visits our home, we require our children to act as social directors for the other children. They are our guests. When they arrive, we sometimes go through a little introduction: "Now, children, these are your guests. I want you to make sure they have a good time."

Then I turn to our guests. "Now, our children are your hosts, and I want you to do whatever they ask you to do." When we have a family over for the first time, I try to talk to the parents beforehand to let them know what's going to happen. I don't want their kids to tell them on the way home, "Mr. and Mrs. Harris said we had to do whatever their kids told us!" I suspect that that might be subject to misinterpretation.

So I say to the parents before the kids come over, "I'm training my children to be hosts, and I'm holding them responsible for entertaining your children. But in order for them to do that, I need your children to cooperate with their plans to show them a good time." When the other parents understand what we're trying to do, they're always supportive.

Unfortunately, what happens in the typical home when guests come over is a far different story. Rather than equipping our kids to be good hosts and giving them the authority to that end, we disarm them and put them at a disadvantage. When little Johnny comes over, we say something like, "You be sure you share with your friend." And in both little minds, that translates into "You have no authority to say no. Little Johnny can do whatever he wants to do." And our child has to stand back and watch Johnny pillage his village.

We should try, instead, to teach our children the responsibilities of both hosts *and* guests. At our house, we give a shortened version of the same lesson to the visiting child when he arrives. While our children and their guests work together toward the goal of having a good time, they also learn accountability and communication skills.

The communication is an important element in what's taking place. Children need to learn to say what they need to say, and to say it with confidence and clarity. In-the-home social interaction helps them develop that ability and boldness which is essential to evangelism.

Now we've come full circle in this discussion, and I trust you've begun to see how teaching hospitality helps our children develop both socially and evangelistically.

Evangelism isn't apologetics, though the two have often been confused in recent years. Apologetics is defending the faith against critics; evangelism is child's play—it's hospitality, extending a loving welcome in Christ's name to friends and neighbors. We don't always have to be on the defense to share our faith.

This has been the work of the Church from its beginning. We read in Acts 2:46-47: "So continuing daily with one accord in the temple, and breaking bread from house to house, they ate their food with gladness and simplicity of heart, praising God and having favor with all the people. And the Lord added to the church daily those who were being saved."

Remember that what children learn by precept and example will stay with them throughout their lives. We can establish households of evangelistic hospitality for generations to come by instilling it in our children. "Train up a child in the way he should go...."

World Missions in Your Home School

The opportunities and learning experiences provided by hospitality aren't limited to reaching friends and relatives. For example, there is a huge mission field of foreign college students in this country—more than 300 thousand of them come every year. Tragically, 90 percent of those students never see the inside of a Christian home; they never experience real hospitality.

Not coincidentally, 90 percent of the foreign students who come here don't like the United States when they leave. My bet is that they're essentially the same group who never receive hospitality. These young people would be able to taste and see that the Lord is good if more Christians would invite them into their homes.

We realize that the potential impact of our evangelistic hospitality is even greater when we look at who those foreign students are. By and large, they're the cream of the crop in their countries. It's estimated that, in each generation, half the leadership of nations around the world will be drawn from men and women who have been trained in the United States. They'll be the elite of their people—doctors, lawyers, engineers, scientists and statesmen. Thus, the opportunity to reach them while they're in college and open to new ideas is enormous. The implications are staggering.

The student you entertain in your home tonight could start a Gospel revolution twenty years from now in a land blinded by the darkness of pagan worship.

Showing hospitality to foreign guests also provides extra educational benefits to our children. A student far from home loves to talk about his family, his way of life, his homeland. And when our kids hear about the history, geography and culture of a foreign land from a native of that land, it's likely to be an unforgettable lesson. They'll never think of that country in the same way again.

When Josh was ten years old, the two of us were visiting the Seattle Space Needle, a huge tower with a revolving restaurant and observation deck at the top. While peering out over the incredible Seattle skyline, we overheard a couple nearby whose accents sounded distinctly British. Being curious, I walked over and asked them where they were from.

"Why, England," they answered.

"Welcome to America!"

"Well, thank you," they said.

I asked if they would be passing through the Portland area, where I live, and they said they would indeed; they were delivering a car from Seattle down to Los Angeles, and then they would be taking another from Los Angeles to Orlando, Florida.

"That's great," I said. "Would you like to come and stay in our home overnight when you pass through Portland?"

They looked at each other. "Thank you, that would be delightful!"

"There's just one catch," I added. "We're teaching my son Joshua at home. Would you be willing to give him a geography and history lesson about England?"

They flashed the biggest grins and said they would be glad to do it. The night they arrived, we shared a pleasurable meal, and the next morning they produced their maps and photo albums. It turned out that they were medical students traveling together and getting to know the "colonies." They gave us a history lesson from Chaucer to Churchill, including an account of the American Revolution from a British perspective. Interesting!

During the course of their brief stay, I also had an opportunity to present the Gospel when our conversation turned to my work and our attempt to school our children from a Biblical world-view. They didn't drop to their knees and make their peace with God, but I could tell their hearts were touched.

I also put them in contact with some other home schoolers across the country, and they stayed with three other Christian families before they made their way back to England. In each place, they heard the Gospel. We've stayed in touch with them, and although I don't know if either has become a Christian yet, one of them did say in a letter that she's now attending church in England. We continue to pray for them.

The Bible charges us to entertain strangers, saying that "by so doing some have unwittingly entertained angels" (Hebrews 13:2). I don't know if our English friends were angels, but I do know that we have a standing invitation to some royal treatment whenever we make our way to England!

Another good way to practice overnight hospitality, especially if you have an older child who's indifferent or even hostile to spiritual things, is to entertain traveling ministers, missionaries and others who have some adventures of faith to tell. Hearing those stories around the table and learning what God is doing throughout the world has a way of kindling faith in a young person's heart.

I'm reminded of the story of Elisha and the Shunammite woman who exercised hospitality every time he passed by (2 Kings 4). One day her son died, and she went to Elisha and asked him to come. When he arrived at her home, Elisha went into the room where the dead boy lay; he stretched himself out on the boy's body, and soon the boy returned to life (2 Kings 4:34-35).

Now that was an extraordinary, miraculous event, but I think there's a general principle in it for us: contact with a holy man or woman of God brings challenge and transformation. He who walks with the wise will be wise. Thus, opening your home to men and women of God and allowing your child to interact with them is one of the most wonderful things you can do for him.

Teaching Stewardship

Another aspect of Christian responsibility we should take steps to instill in our children is the stewardship of our livelihood and our money. There are several principles parents should understand and teach in the laboratory of Christian family life.

First, we read in Proverbs 22:7, "The rich rule over the poor, and the borrower is servant to the lender." I interpret that verse to mean that God wants us to meet our obligations and to provide for our families (see 1 Timothy 5:8) without incurring commercial, interest-bearing, debt. Being in debt to anyone, even without usury, is a form of bondage, but being in debt to a bank is a legal form of modern slavery. Your local banker "loves you and has a wonderful plan for your life", and you're not going to like it. You will spend most of your time making your master wealthier while you struggle to stay afloat.

The majority of Americans today are spending everything they earn and more, piling up debt and living from paycheck to paycheck. They're always on the brink of financial disaster. There is no room for making a mistake. But, God calls us to live within our incomes and set aside for emergencies, as well. If we don't obey this principle and teach it to our children, where will they learn it? Certainly not from the bankers.

Second, we read in Deuteronomy 8:18, "It is God who is giving you power to make wealth." The ability to serve is the ability to create wealth. People are designed to serve God and one another. Everyone can serve in some way or another. Everyone can provide services to others in ways that allow them to receive the things they need in life. The Sovereign God who created us also requires us to provide for our families. And if anyone will not work, neither shall he eat. In other words, our ability to serve others in our work is all the ability we need to create the income we need to fulfill our obligations. God works in partnership with us.

Understanding those two principles, we need to teach our kids the patience and self-denial to provide for their families without debt, as well as the skills that allow them, with God's help, to do honorable, skillful work. Even though we don't have a right to be employed by another, we always have the ability and responsibility to work. We can meet our obligations through family business activities. By family business, I mean all manner of entrepreneurial activities that are pursued by and for the good of the family. This can include outside hourly employment, but it doesn't have to. We can teach our children how to be employers, who create good, well-paying jobs for others.

In order for that to happen, we first have to teach them how to "see." Opportunities abound. There's always some kind of need that we can meet in a mutually profitable way, some kind of work we can do, some kind of service we can provide, some new line of products we can take to those who need it. In other words, there's always some kind of business venture we can start. Our children will never need to worry about "finding a job" if they are willing to avoid commercial debt and learn to be self-motivated, self-directed and self-employed. Employers will line up to pay top dollar for such workers, but more important, such workers will not need an employer to set up their work for them. They can turn the boss into just another client.

As for our future stay-at-home mothers, prepare them to be versatile, highly skilled assistants to their future self-employed or professional husbands. Office machine and computer skills will be useful, no matter what their family business may turn out to be. At the very least, our daughters can learn to be better managers of the resources in hand. Home economics and the ability to stretch a dollar are important parts of any household.

Entrepreneurial Stewardship

Our children should be taught to work hard while they're young. They should bear the yoke of responsibility in their early teens, investing and reinvesting most of what they earn back into the family business venture so they will have a family that can assist them in launching their own household when they are ready to marry and have a family. I call this "Home Banking." By saving aggressively and spending the savings only in ways that increase productivity and and income, the family can quickly become a solid financial platform from which to launch new families. If a young person follows this course, he'll enjoy the great freedom of knowing that his fate does not rest in the hands of an employer or in a fickle international economy.[2]

My name for this approach is "entrepreneurial stewardship." It means taking the initiative to seek and use financial opportunities for God's purpose. Supported with a bit of good parental advice, it can lead to some interesting and very rewarding work for a young person.

A sixteen-year-old boy in Dallas, for example, wanted to make money during the summer to pay for a college education. A common story, right? And, like most young people in his situation, when he went out looking for a job, the best he could find was flipping hamburgers in a fast-food restaurant.

Fortunately, this boy's father was an accountant who worked with small businesses, and he suggested to his son that he run his own business for the summer. "But what can I do?" the son asked.

"I don't know," his father answered. "What have you done to make money in past summers?"

"Well, I can mow lawns."

When I was a kid, having a lawn-moving business meant you went into the garage, got out Dad's mower, filled it with gas, and started knocking on doors until you found someone willing to pay to have his lawn mowed. You could make twenty-five to thirty dollars a week, or even more, if you worked like a horse.

This enterprising father-son team put their heads together and came up with a better way. Instead of just mowing lawns, they started a lawn mowing business. First, the boy had letterhead stationery printed with "Lawns of Dallas" at the top. Next, with his dad's typewriter, he wrote letters of inquiry to all the businesses in his area that had large lawns. He offered to mow their lawns as often as needed throughout the summer for one flat fee. "We'll negotiate the price, and you'll give me fifty percent down and the rest at the end of the summer if you're satisfied with my work," he wrote.

After mailing his letters, he put on his suit, borrowed his dad's briefcase and car, and called on all the people to whom he had written. There's something about a kid that age, who is showing such initiative, that makes you want to see him succeed. And succeed he did. He walked in to see these businessmen, and walked out with signed contracts in hand.

He did so well in selling his service that he drew a lot of accounts away from professional lawn-care companies. There was a lot more work to do than this young man could possible do alone. So he hired some of his friends who hadn't found summer work and had them start mowing his clients' lawns with their own mowers. The net result? At the end of the summer, after paying his employees a better wage than they could find anywhere else, he had ten thousand dollars profit in the bank. Not bad for a summer job!

Now my point in recounting this story is not to put dollar signs in anyone's eyes. It is simply to illustrate that there is more potential in starting a small company than in getting a job. In his book, *How to Make Big Money Mowing Small Lawns*, Robert Welcome points out that this kind of success is not unreasonable at all, provided the mowing business is handled as a real business. Teenagers can be very successful with just a little coaching from parents. If a teen has enough time to spend on starting up, and has access to good counsel, he or she can get ahead fast in a small business venture. The old adage that it takes money to make money is true only to a point. When it comes to teenage entrepreneurs, I have seen some very short "shoestring" budgets succeed.

At this point, I can hear someone murmuring that "Over 80% of all new businesses fail." That is simply not true. In fact, according to the latest and most credible statistics, nearly 70% of companies formed in 1985 were still alive nine years later in 1994. Of those that were out of business, only about 18% ended in real failure where creditors lost money. The rest were closed down voluntarily for various reasons.[1]

Even if the failure rates of new businesses were higher, we must take into account the fact that most new businesses immediately borrow as much money as they can from commercial sources in order to act like an established company before they can really afford to. When you read that such and such a business "failed," you are reading the business "obituary." Read the business "autopsy" and you may discover that the business was actually murdered by impatient creditors who removed all of its vital organs just before it died. Rather than wait for an otherwise sound business to improve its cash-flow, these lenders have removed the equipment and receivables to get what they can out of their "bad investment." Contracts allow commercial lenders serve as the judge, jury, executioner, and undertaker of the failed business. "The borrower becomes servant to the lender."

Never borrow money from anyone who loves money more than he loves you. And one sure sign is the requirement of interest or usery. A legitimate "family loan" is interest free and the payment schedule is determined by the need to make the same funds available for loaning out, interest free to other members of the family. A strong cluster of debt-free households in service to God is better by far than an interest-bearing savings account.

Home Business Strategy

I have researched this topic and presented my findings in some detail in The Home & Family Business Workshop. The tapes of that workshop offer a complete orientation to getting started in a family business. If you feel led to start such a venture with your family, it would be helpful to order and listen to those tapes and read at least one good book on the subject of family business [2]. Then sit down with your spouse and your children to determine the field you are interested in working in and what kind of small business you could start in that field that could involve all the members of your family above age ten. The strategy to follow when starting a family business is simple and straightforward.

First, pick your field, not your business. A field is a broad area of business, such as construction, education, or entertainment. In every field there are innumerable opportunities to serve others and therefore to make an income. Certain skills, such as trucking, data entry and graphic arts are involved in every field. A self-employed truck driver can choose to haul anything from toxic waste to lawn furniture. By choosing your field you decide what kinds of people and products you want to serve. If it is a field you enjoy and which is worthwhile for reasons other than profit you will enjoy your work more and need fewer breaks and vacations to get away from it.

It is alarming how many adults today hate their work. It doesn't have to be that way. If we will only be more careful in picking our field, we could have a much more interesting and enjoyable career, even if we are doing basically the same kind of work. One way to identify a field you might enjoy working in is to ask the question, "What would I do if I didn't have to do anything to make money?" Be honest. If the answer is "I'd hike." or "I'd paint." or even, "I'd play baseball." you are tipping yourself off to the kinds of people and products you might enjoy working with. You may not have the skill to play professional baseball, but you might be able to produce sports related gifts and clothing. You may not be able to get paid for hiking, but you may be able to start a mail order company selling the latest in hiking gear. The result is you will know which trade shows to attend for ideas and information. If you hate toxic waste, you might enjoy being one of the modern day heroes who help to clean up our environment, and make a very well deserved income to boot, or you may wish to avoid the field altogether. Either way, pick your field before you go any farther or you may end up as a miserable employee in a business you own.

Second, get counsel. After listening to the tapes and reading the books, you should seek out local advisors. Take a Christian attorney, a Christian accountant and a successful Christian businessman out for lunch, one at a time. Prepare your questions carefully. And pay for their lunch! There are a lot of additional resources available, including many brethren who have been successful as entrepreneurs themselves—they're usually glad to share the wisdom they've gained from experience. You may have to travel far away to get people involved in your specific line of work to talk to you openly. Local businesses in the same field may fear competition.

Third, once you've picked your field and collected some business ideas that look interesting, take inventory. What kind of capital or discretionary income do you have to invest in a business of your own? Realize there's a risk involved in starting any new business, and don't commit money you can't afford to lose. Don't mortgage your home or other assets. Sell them if you think it makes sense to do so. If God is with you, your "shoestring budget" will always be enough to take the next step. And when the money is not there, God is probably saying "Wait." When the timing is right, and you have been doing your homework, you will have both the knowledge and the resources to take the necessary action.

Also, consider what talents, experience, and training you and your family have. Of the businesses which interest you, which ones would build on those personal assets? Be realistic. If you have never worked with wood, how can you be sure you will be able to make a salable product? Likewise, consider how much time you and your family can invest in a business. Some business opportunities like finished-craft making consume a lot of time in both production and marketing; others, like craft-kit design, manufacture and wholesale, are actually more profitable and don't require as much time, even though they are in the same basic field.

Fourth, honor the laws of the land. When you look into the legal side of your business you may run into zoning laws, product safety laws and other requirements that can seem like a brick wall. "What?! I have to have an industrial oven just in order to bake brownies for sale?" Don't be dismayed. Where there's a will there's a way. You may not be able to do everything exactly the way you had hoped. Its called "red tape." But with a little flexibility, you can still succeed. And remember, the more difficult it is for you to get through these legal hurdles, the more difficult it will be for others to follow you into the business and become your competition. That is why established businesses are sometimes in favor of these expensive laws. They protect the bigger companies by discouraging start-ups. And the claims of product safety and environmental safety are sometimes valid. You wouldn't want to poison anyone with your brownies, would you? If God is with you, you can meet the standards, obey all the laws and still be profitable.

Finally, take action. Out of 100 people today, only 67 are likely to have established goals. Of those 67, only 10 are likely to have made practical plans. And of those 10, only two are able to follow through and take action. The noble man makes noble plans and by noble deeds he stands (Isaiah 32:8). Be part of the two percent who take forceful action toward your goals to start a family business.

Taking action may mean filing for a vendor's license in your state. With a business license you can buy materials at a discount from wholesalers. It also protects the use of the name you and your family have chosen for your business. Over ten years ago my own family went through this process, and became recognized as the Harris Family Business in the State of Oregon. We focus primarily on publishing and producing the materials for my workshops. But Josh now has his own distinct business called New Attitude under which he publishes New Attitude magazine and presents New Attitude conferences for parents and teenagers. The apple doesn't fall far from the tree.

Be sure to develop a marketing strategy for whatever business you intend to pursue, and test it before committing a lot of time, effort, and money. The Dallas teenager's strategy, for instance, was to send out letters on his letterhead to prospective clients, then follow up with personal visits. If no one bought his service, he had little to lose. Take your time and grow slowly. There are no leaps of faith in the kingdom of God, only steps of faith.

History and Storytelling

One final, critical element of building Christian character in the laboratory of family life is storytelling. Because of the form of modern education, most of us are used to learning historical facts in a plain, colorless way. But that's not the way we learn and remember best. We need the drama of storytelling. So do our children.

Not accidentally, most of the Bible consists of stories showing the history of how God relates to man, and vice versa, and we rob ourselves and our children if we concentrate only on New Testament epistles. God gives us, not only commandments, but also real-life examples of how He expects His people to respond to them. God's stories, you see, confront us with the consequences of life's most basic choice—to obey or disobey Him. His stories instill in us the necessary motivation to fear Him. Thus, whenever a person *doesn't* know God's stories, he will not keep God's commandments. It's that simple.

Listen, O my people, to my instruction; incline your ears to the words of my mouth. I will open my mouth in a parable; I will utter dark sayings of old, which we have heard and known, and our fathers have told us. We will not conceal them from their children, but tell to the generation to come the praises of the Lord, and His strength and His wondrous works that He has done. For He established a testimony in Jacob, and appointed a law in Israel, which He commanded our fathers, that they should teach them to their children, that the generation to come might know, even the children yet to be born, that they may arise and tell them to their children, that they should put their confidence in God, and not forget the works of God, and keep His commandments (Psalm 78:1-7).

The prerequisite to effective action is affective motivation, something that touches the heart and attitude. We can say to a child over and over, "You shall not steal," for example. But until we tell a story that shows the bad things that happen to thieves, we haven't touched the heart, and we haven't motivated the child to obey.

The time to tell our stories is as soon as our kids can understand, *before* they have to make tough decisions, and *before* they're caught in a situation in which they lose their ability to think clearly and objectively.

There are three types of stories we need to tell our children to mold their hearts: (1) stories from our own experience, (2) Bible stories, and (3) stories of our national heritage. Let's look briefly at each.

One woman told me about her mother, who used personal experience stories with great wisdom and effectiveness. She said, "When I was ten years old, my mom came in and sat down on the edge of my bed. 'Honey,' she said, 'in a few years you're going to be a teenager, and a lot of teenagers go through a period where they feel like they're grown up, but they're really not. And they want to make all the decisions in their lives, but they're not really wise enough or experienced enough to do that. So sometimes in those cases, there's a tension between a mother and her daughter. Now, that happened to me when I was a teenager. Let me tell you about it...'"

The mother told her story, and that girl of ten soaked it in, even though she didn't believe it at the time. Later, however, when she felt those same feelings, she realized, "I'm acting just like Mom said I would." Knowing that, helped her keep herself in check and sail relatively smoothly through what could have been a tempest.

When the girl turned sixteen, before she started seeing boys, her mother told her about her own experiences with boys and dating, and the lessons she had learned. Later still, when the girl married, the mother told her stories and lessons of her marriage, lessons immensely helpful to the young bride. She did the same when the young woman prepared to have her first child.

Finally, shortly before I talked to this woman, her mother called one more time. "Do you know what she wanted to talk about?" the woman asked me. "Menopause."

Notice that this wise mother didn't tell her ten-year-old daughter about menopause. At each stage of the girl's life, she told her about the stage that was coming next. She told her what she needed to hear at the time. Notice also that she didn't preach or poke her nose in where it didn't belong. She told the stories of her own life, trusting her daughter to heed their lessons while recognizing that all of us make our own share of mistakes.

Bible stories, likewise, provide a rich heritage for us to draw upon, and we need to work through them regularly with our children. Catherine Voss's *Child's Story Bible* has always been my favorite volume. Bible stories show human nature at its best and its worst, often with painful honesty. They also show us the nature of God. Because the Bible stories are part of God's inspired Word, hearing and learning them equips us for holy living in all areas of life.

In your search for appropriate Bible stories for your children, (and not all are appropriate for all ages) don't overlook some of the more obscure Bible characters. For every famous hero like David there are many little known characters like Ahimaaz, the courier found in 2 Sam. 18. The lessons to be learned in the little stories are tremendous. Consider the example of poor Ahimaaz. The story takes place during the time when old King David was hiding out in the wilderness. His army was fighting against the insurrection of David's own son, Absalom. Unbeknownst to David, General Joab has killed the King's son, and so the battle is over. All that is left to be done is to send the news to the elderly king.

At this point, a young athletic type named Ahimaaz, the son of Zadok the Priest, said to Joab, "Let me run and take the news to the king that the LORD has delivered him from the hand of his enemies."

"You are not the one to take the news today," Joab told him. "You may take the news another time, but you must not do so today, because the king's son is dead." Joab is doing the young man a favor.

Then Joab said to an unnamed courier who, we are told, was a Cushite, "Go, tell the king what you have seen." The Cushite bowed down before Joab and ran off. The message was simply what the Cushite had observed. David is still king because the king's rebellious son is dead. There was no specific wording provided by General Joab.

But Ahimaaz is aching for action. Again he said to Joab, "Come what may, please let me run behind the Cushite." But Joab replied, "My son, why do you want to go? You don't have any news that will bring you a reward."

But Ahimaaz responded, "Come what may, I want to run."

So Joab said, "Run!"

Now Ahimaaz had his chance to show his stuff! He was by far the faster runner, but he also knew a short cut to David's camp. We are told that he ran by way of the plain and outran the Cushite. When he arrived at David's camp, Ahimaaz called out to the king, "All is well!" He bowed down before the king with his face to the ground and said, "Praise be to the LORD your God! He has delivered up the men who lifted their hands against my lord the king."

As a loving father, rebellious or not, David's heart was concerned for the safety of his son. He asked, "Is the young man Absalom safe?" The answer that Ahimaaz gave should be posted as a banner over the head of many a talented young man in the ministry today. "I saw great confusion... but I don't know what it was."

Can you imagine the old king's amazement? Why run all that way if you don't have the message? Why not just wait until you have something to say? Speed and smarts do not create the calling. But David was very patient with the young athlete. He simply asked Ahimaaz to, "Stand aside and wait here."

Then the Cushite came jogging into camp. He wasn't very fast. Maybe he wasn't very smart. But he had the message. He understood what he had seen, and he gave the king the news he feared. Absalom was dead. So David went up to the room over the gateway and wept.

There will be times in every young person's life when stories like this can make the difference between making a right decision and making a wrong decision. Bible stories speak to our hearts, and they have so much to teach us.

Finally, we have a national heritage worth knowing, one we and our children must understand if we're to make wise decisions in this Republic of ours in the years ahead. Hearing how the Pilgrims and other founders lived and believed would help us learn what should be done about the federal budget deficits. Hearing the story of Patrick Henry, who rallied the colonists to fight for independence, would help us remember the importance of a strong national defense. Telling the story of George Washington and his many close encounters with death on the battle field impress upon us that when God is with us, we need not fear. We can have confidence that God's plan will be brought to completion.

In telling these stories of our Nation's past, however, let's not be so zealous in correcting the abuses of liberal historians that we create our own historical revisionism. If the Founding Fathers were alive today, some of them would not want to go to the typical Evangelical church. Some were influenced by the pagan Enlightenment, as well as the Protestant Reformation.

One historical figure (not a Founding Father) who's been misrepresented in our quest to find Christian heroes is Johnny Appleseed. He's routinely pictured as a nice man who went around scattering apple seeds everywhere and toting a Bible under his arm. The fact is, Johnny Appleseed was a missionary for Swedenborgism, a spiritist cult. This cult taught many false doctrines and claimed that the writings of the Apostle Paul had no place in the Bible. When a child hears that Johnny Appleseed is a "godly hero" and then discovers that he was in fact a cult member, what will he logically conclude about everything else he's been taught? Good scholarship and honesty are needed in handling history. Don't be so desperate for godly heroes that you teach things that are not true.

Our stories also have to acknowledge that God's plan for His people is not always easy. He brought the Pilgrims safely to Plymouth Rock, but many of them died during their first winter in the New World. Yet, it was clearly due to God's grace that any of them survived. So let's get our history right and tell our kids stories they can trust. The real history tests they take will not be on paper.

Let's also recapture the reason for holidays. A holiday is not just a day off from work so we can go to the beach or have a picnic. Holidays are meant, rather, to be times for remembering, times for telling stories, honoring the elderly and instructing the young. On birthdays, celebrate the rich life of the person being honored by telling stories about him or her through the years. On church holidays, keep the focus on the birth, death and resurrection of Christ. Don't lose the heart of the holidays. On Memorial Day, children need to hear about fathers and uncles and grandfathers who fought in wars, even giving their lives to preserve the freedom we enjoy today. On the Fourth of July, they need to hear of the courage and resolve of men who gladly put their lives on the line to establish a nation "conceived in liberty and dedicated to the proposition that all men are created equal." Tell these things to your children.

Finding Time for Storytelling

Television is perhaps the greatest enemy of storytelling today. When the tube goes on, all conversation stops. When it appeared in America, the front porch swing disappeared. It's time for us to take a second look and determine how to best use our time.

Storytelling isn't something we do only at designated times. As we read in Deuteronomy, chapter 6, we should be teaching throughout every day—as we're out walking, as we're driving in a car, as we're getting the children dressed in the morning. We should tell stories about the fish we've caught, the tree houses we've built, the dolls we loved, the honesty of Abraham Lincoln, the way Jesus sought out the sinful tax collector named Zaccheus, and so on. There is plenty of time to tell these stories. There is just not enough time for watching television.

Summary

Our homes can be embassies of the Kingdom of God; our family members can be ambassadors for Christ. Church growth statistics suggest that 70 to 80 percent of new Christians are won by friends and relatives. They are won in the laboratory of Christian family life.

That laboratory begins at home with hospitality. Christian hospitality trains children to build healthy social skills. It also puts a whole new and exciting mission field right in our living rooms and guest rooms.

The laboratory of family life extends to our pocketbooks as well.

Parents need to teach their children principles of entrepreneurial stewardship. Children need to learn that everything they have is a gift from God. He obligates them to use those gifts to His glory. They should also learn that skillful work is part of God's plan. Let's encourage our children to be faithful entrepreneurs and frugal homemakers.

Finally, the laboratory of family life needs to be remembered and shared. Its story must be told. Thus, we ought to tell stories in our homes. Our lives are full of them. The Bible is, too. Our lives are, too. And our nation has a story worth telling. We rob our children if we feed them only Romans and the Westminster Catechism. Let's not just tell your children not to steal. Let's tell them a story of what happens to those who do. Let's be accurate and honest in the way we handle history.

The laboratory of Christian family life is where home schooling really spreads its wings and takes flight. Let's be sure to use these "lab courses" faithfully.

Stand not alone, dear friend, 'tis much too windy and cold. The warmth and fellowship of two cuts the torrents and seals the breeze as none else.

Tristram Gylberd

SUPPORT GROUPS

The story of Elijah's victory over the priests of Baal on Mount Carmel is one of the most thrilling in the entire Bible (1 Kings 18). Picture those 450 pagan priests setting up their altar, making their sacrifices, and calling out to their false god hour after hour, all to no avail. Frustrated, they reached deep into their perverted bag of tricks and brought out swords and lances with which to mutilate themselves in an attempt to show Baal how serious and devout they were. Alas, Baal didn't listen. He sent no fire to consume their sacrifice.

Then Elijah built his altar, made his sacrifice and arranged it on the altar. Next, he soaked it with water three times. Finally he prayed, asking God to accept the sacrifice and demonstrate His power again to the people of Israel. "Then the fire of the Lord fell, and consumed the burnt offering and the wood and the stones and the dust" (1 Kings 18:38). What a fire! What a scene!

As if that weren't enough for one business trip, Elijah next slew all the priests of Baal and then prayed for rain, which God miraculously supplied. It poured.

Now, after all that, you'd think Elijah would have been emotionally and spiritually exhilarated. Could he have asked for more proof of the presence and power of the Lord, as well as His blessing on his life and ministry? But that's not the way the story goes. Instead, Elijah fell victim to what has become popularly known as "The Elijah Syndrome."

Shortly after his great victories, Elijah found himself threatened by evil Queen Jezebel. He was so frightened he ran for his life. He hid in a cave and there announced to God, "I have been very zealous for the Lord, the God of hosts; for the sons of Israel have forsaken Thy covenant, torn down Thine altars and killed Thy prophets with the sword. And I alone am left; and they seek my life, to take it away" (1 Kings 19:10). Elijah was depressed because he thought he was all alone. But God encouraged him by revealing that there were seven thousand others who had not bowed their knee to Baal. God also arranged immediately for Elijah to have a young protégé, Elisha, to follow him and to learn from him.

It's a natural human tendency whenever we hurt or struggle to think we're all alone in the world; that no one else has experienced our pain or could understand our trials. It happens to the most devout people, even to prophets of God. And the solution is fellow-ship and responsibility for others in God's family.

As a home schooler, you can find yourself feeling that way often. On the heels of a great breakthrough in teaching, the program is suddenly not working as smoothly as you'd hoped. Perhaps your child is challenging your authority. Friends and relatives may think you're strange to have pulled your child out of the conventional schools. It can seem a lonely experience, even when your motives are the best. The Elijah Syndrome strikes home.

Fortunately, as with Elijah, God is providing fellowship for you. Growing right along with the popularity of home school is the home-schooling support group. Support groups will fill the void—before the Elijah Syndrome sets in.

No Home School is an Island

home-school support groups are made up of parents who are educating their own children. Thus, we'll find peers in these groups, not "professionals." The group meetings and conferences benefit their members in a number of ways.

First, they provide emotional support. There is tremendous encouragement in getting together and trading curriculum ideas, anecdotes and "war stories" with others who have the same mission. By hearing that others experience the same problems and frustrations, as well as the same joys and sense of accomplishment, we can overcome that awful sense of isolation and loneliness. Just getting together reminds us of the common bond we share. It reassures us that what we're doing is good and right.

Second, home-school support groups provide an opportunity to learn from one another's experiences. Ideally, each group has a mixture of experienced and novice home schoolers. That way, chances are better that someone in the group has a good answer to whatever questions are raised.

For example, if one parent is looking for a good science project, another member or two will likely have a suggestion. If a parent is struggling with discipline, others should be able to say how they handled the same situation with their children.

Third, support groups make possible the group activities that need to be part of any schooling experience, including home schooling: field trips. Field trips are usually best taken in small groups of one or two families. Larger groups can become a "cattle drive" in which all the children just wander through the museum or nature center, while all the parents are enjoying "fellowship" at the back of the herd. This is not educationally effective. Better to have an adult hand on every child's shoulder, directing his attention and answering questions.

Special rates on going to the symphony can be gained through a large association of home-school support groups. Ski trips, visits to places such as Sea World or Plymouth Plantation, and other educational outings in your region sometimes need volume in order to be affordable. That is one advantage of a support group.

Fourth, by pooling financial resources, support groups make possible such co-op activities as science labs and paid instructors for art, music, ballet and team sports. There are now home-school marching bands, oil painting co-ops, rocketry clubs and ski clubs. Every year a National Home School Basketball Tournament is held in Colorado Springs. Ask around, and you may start a club or co-op to meet your students' interests.

Fifth, support groups can provide adult education—training for the parents in how to be better teachers, both in general and in specific subjects, such as reading and math. My own workshops are hosted by support groups across the United States and overseas, either live or on video tape. The Basic Home-Schooling Workshop has been used successfully to kick off the establishment of state Christian Home Education Associations and metropolitan support groups. Once established, many of these groups serve as our annual workshop hosts.

Sixth, when support groups are made up of people of like faith, they can also provide spiritual support for the members. As in all such fellowships, this support goes far beyond mere socializing by helping members draw on God's resources, as well as their own. I recommend that Christian groups remain such, but they should also be ready to help all families find their own style of support in the area. We can do good to all men, but especially to those of the household of faith. Be a good neighbor to all home-schooling families, regardless of other differences.

Finally, support group associations at the state level are usually involved in political action, lobbying their legislatures for helpful bills and otherwise working to secure the rights of all home schoolers. These state associations need the full support of all kinds of home-schooling families. When there are several associations, they should form a state coalition to coordinate their activities.

For all these reasons, we need to become active in a local support group. Those of us in this movement need to stick together and stand up for each other. We also need to build each other up. As Mary Pride has said,

Home schoolers who fail to tap into this rich source are not only denying themselves many wonderful opportunities, but are failing to support the sacrificial efforts of those who are working to make home schooling legal and respectable. Obviously, the more numbers a state group can claim, the more impact it can have on legislators and the media. Stand up and be counted![1]

One group of home schoolers in the Houston area has the ideal support group—their church! Twelve home-schooling families have been gathering at the church building every Friday for several years. In the beginning, they took a field trip on those days, and the pastor taught the children their catechism. More recently, they've whetted their children's appetites for fine arts. One year, the students were taught art and art history; the next year, music appreciation and theory. Students also learn sign language.

The only support group we should ever need for Christian living is our own local church. The Christian education program should teach parents how to teach any subject to their children. The church library should be well-equipped with books, tapes, and videos for this purpose. When this happens, it makes the role of the church that much more effective in "equipping the saints for the work of the ministry."

In years to come, we can expect more support groups to develop within local churches, and this is a good thing. However, we must not get out of touch with the home-schooling community beyond our church fellowship. Legislative issues require state-wide communication of news. Rallies at the state capitol must be well attended. State conventions must grow larger if we are to resist the attempts of the National Education Association to curb the rights of home-schooling parents.

Another excellent source of support for home-schooling families is the local Christian school. For a small, reasonable fee you can enjoy annual testing of your students, access to a complete library of Christian literature, extracurricular sports, assemblies, band, choir, science lab courses, higher math classes, art classes, and the counsel of experienced Christian teachers. I have personally helped some of the largest Christian schools in the United States establish these "home school extension services." They work very well if parents and school administrators are willing to be supportive of one another. A tuition of 25 percent of the normal school tuition is usually fair. Additional fees may be added for sports or band. If you have a Christian school nearby, ask them if they are willing to work with you.

Levels of Support

Support groups exist at several levels across the country. In a given locale, you may be part of five different levels of organization.

The first and most numerous, of course, are the local, or neighborhood, groups made up of parents who live near each other. Ideally, these groups include five or six families. That usually translates into twelve to sixteen kids! If a group gets larger than this, field trips become less an educational experience and more a cattle drive, as already mentioned.

It's possible for local support groups to be made up entirely of people from the same church, and that's probably the most convenient arrangement if it can be worked out. The members of a support group may even constitute a Sunday school class. This has worked quite well in many churches.

The second level is the district, in which several local groups get together for larger activities, such as park days. It's at this level that there are likely to be sufficient resources available to pay for co-op classes in music, science lab, ballet and so on.

The third level is the city-wide group, which would cover an entire metropolitan area. At this level, besides political activity, you'll find state conventions that not only bring people together from across the country, but also provide an opportunity for curriculum publishers and other home-school suppliers to display their wares and answer your questions.

Finally, on the national level, you have several sources of support. There are national publications, like *The Teaching Home*, *Practical Homeschooling*, and *Homeschooling Today*. Advertisers can reach a national audience of home-schooling families through these magazines. You also have national organizations, like Noble Publishing Associates, which publishes materials especially for use by home-schooling families; and Christian Life Workshops, which conducts training workshops and seminars. A few state Christian home-school associations have now gained a national profile because of the quality of their organization and services. California, Texas and New York's organizations have had influence beyond their own state borders.

It is not unusual for a family to be introduced to home-schooling by a national organization. However, a national ministry cannot provide the day-to-day support you will need. Only a friendly face and a gentle voice in your own community can do that. So please, when you call any national service, ask for a contact number for you to get in touch with your local groups. If you don't have one, start one.

Starting a Local Support Group

If there is currently no local support group in your area, and you want to help start one, proceed carefully. First, if the group is to have a Christian orientation, it needs to be founded on some documents that spell out what the members believe and that address some of the obvious problems that are likely to arise in the years ahead. There's a tendency whenever friends start something—be it a support group or a business or a church—to think that contracts or charters or statements of faith aren't necessary. And, indeed, those founding documents are unimportant—until something goes wrong. A disagreement over policy or doctrine or an aggressive intruder can mean a lot of problems for the group. Know who you are and what you stand for when you begin. Then you'll know what to do to protect the group.

A statement of faith, which should be affirmed by any potential group leader, ought to be broad enough to include Christians who disagree on nonessential matters (such as eschatology), but narrow enough to exclude people from a nonevangelical framework or who hold abhorrent opinions. Many groups have found that the statement used by the Association of Christian Schools International serves their purposes well.

There are two particular groups of people who have a history of trying to join Christian support groups and move into leadership under false pretenses. The first of these are white supremacists, many of whom are involved in neo-Nazi or survivalist groups. These people are usually motivated to pursue home schooling out of a desire to isolate their children from those of other races. The body of Christ will include members from every tongue, tribe, and nation. To keep these people out, your group needs a clear anti-racism statement in its charter. As the economy staggers under huge deficits and high taxes, these groups tend to grow. As the bombing in Oklahoma in 1995 demonstrates, these people can be dangerous.

The second group seeking admittance in increasing numbers to local support groups are homosexual and lesbian parents. God's Word clearly condemns these sexual perversions. Again, to keep these people out, you need a clear statement in the founding documents.

Both of these groups are attracted to home schooling because they have been socially isolated and often persecuted. They seem to assume that home schoolers are kindred spirits because of the legal battles related to home education. Needless to say, Christian home schoolers have little in common with such people, but we need to say so. In three different programs, I heard home schooling mentioned in connection with the Oklahoma City bombing and the militia movements. If a group's charter doesn't contain clear statements barring racists and homosexuals *before* they try to enter, a group can easily become embattled and split. Personal feelings of compassion and a decision to help such people should not be confused with group policy. Respond to them on a personal level, but keep them out of the group.

Even among Christians, a support group can run into trouble if just one member forgets the group's purpose and tries to turn it into a doctrinal battleground. People with strong views about things, such as eschatology, should form groups with like-minded people, rather than disrupt the peace of other groups. And all groups should strive to stick to the purpose at hand, which isn't sectarian. If you intend to be a Christian group, put "Christian" in your name. It will save you a lot of debate later on.

Now, by warning you to be prepared in your founding documents to exclude clearly incompatible people from your group, I don't mean to imply that Christian home schoolers should have nothing to do with non-Christians. We can be good neighbors without becoming entangled. Also note that there is a difference between the <u>local</u> group meeting in your living room, and the larger associations and coalitions that meet in public halls. There are certainly common concerns on which we can meet, such as lobbying for the rights of parents to home school. However, for spiritual support, you and other like-minded Christians will clearly need to meet together in homes or churches as a separate group. Your children shouldn't have to discuss with other children who they were in a past life. (This has happened!) Nor should race or sexual orientation be an issue of discussion.

It goes almost without saying (but is too important to ignore) that you should not join a group or take part in any activity that would force you to compromise on crucial matters of Christian doctrine. That's always too high a price to pay for getting along with others (2 Corinthians 6:14-18). We can cooperate for a worthy cause, but we should try not to get entangled in the affairs of unbelieving families. Again, respond to needs personally, or in the name of your church, not as a home-school support group.

The Nehemiah Balance

It's also possible, especially in areas where there are legal struggles involved in home schooling, for a group to become preoccupied with the legal and political issues and to ignore the other reasons for working together. Some groups are so politically active that they are of no educational good. Others are so educationally oriented that they bury their heads in textbooks and don't see the political battle brewing in their state. The model to follow here is that of Nehemiah, who directed the rebuilding of the walls of Jerusalem despite fierce and potentially violent opposition. He instructed his men to continue working at the task to which they had been called, wielding a tool in one hand and a weapon in the other, in case the enemy attacked. That is "The Nehemiah Balance."

Lessons for Leaders

If you lead a support group, or if you think you ever might, or if you want to give some good advice to your current leaders, here is a plan to circumvent growing pains before they strike.

Many groups get into trouble because they're unprepared for success. As I've said before, the home-school movement is exploding, so most support groups grow rapidly. Leaders need to learn early how to delegate responsibility and spur all the members to share the burden, financially and otherwise.

In the beginning, you may be glad to put out the newsletter (paying the postage yourself), make all the calls and organize all the activities. But ask yourself what the situation will be like when the need for everything—time, effort, and money—is *tripled*. If you couldn't handle that, then begin to plan *now*! Put the group on a sound financial footing. Make every activity pay for itself. Door charges, subscriptions and membership dues should be set high enough to allow the quality to improve over time.

Also, learn how to delegate. If you don't begin to delegate, your duties within the group will eventually detract from your primary responsibilities: the training of your own children and the care of your own family. The exhilaration of being a new leader can evaporate quickly when you see your family life eroding. I've seen good leaders drop out in frustration, all for failure to anticipate growth.

When you delegate a responsibility to another person, don't take it back just because you know you could do it better. Remember that your first efforts weren't the best either, and that you learned and improved with experience. Give the other person that same chance. Eventually, with your advice, they may get *better* than you.

Hanging Together

When the Declaration of Independence had been signed, back in 1776, Benjamin Franklin said to the other delegates, "Gentlemen, we must hang together, or we shall all hang separately." The same might be said of those of us who are involved in home schooling our children. We have a tremendous opportunity to shape our children into arrows that will be mighty weapons in the hand of God, but the task isn't easy, and there are obstacles, legal and otherwise, along the way. By becoming active in support groups, however, we don't have to walk alone.

Summary

Home schoolers may often find themselves feeling alone in the face of opposition. It needn't be that way.

Support groups for home schoolers help meet a number of needs. They provide emotional support. They provide opportunities for sharing experience and wisdom. They make group activities possible. By pooling money and resources, support groups can sponsor science labs and hire teachers for art, music and sports. Support groups can provide adult education to train parents to be better teachers. When the groups are made up of people of like faith, they can spiritually nourish the members. State level groups are usually involved in lobbying efforts.

There is no need to stand alone. Join a group or, if need be, start a group. Adventures like home schooling are best enjoyed when they are shared.

TAKING THE PLUNGE

The people of Israel had endured in Egyptian slavery for more than 350 years. They were beaten and abused. They were poorly fed, clothed and housed. Their taskmasters kept them under hard labor in the hope that the Israelites would never have the time or energy to realize that they were "more and mightier" than the Egyptians themselves (Exodus 1:9). The *mentality* of their bondage was stronger than their chains.

Then one day, the Pharaoh of Egypt grew so concerned with the population of slaves that he ordered the Hebrew midwives to kill all the male children who were being born. The midwives tricked the king and refused to obey him. God honored the midwives who feared the Lord by giving them children of their own. Evidently, civil disobedience has its proper time and place. In frustration, Pharaoh commanded Hebrew parents themselves to do the killing. As slaves, most parents simply obeyed. It was the Law.

But one particular son was born to a man from the tribe of Levi. The child's mother wanted to save him, so she hid him. After three months, however, she could hide him no longer, and her great faith in God, which had led her to protect the innocent child, could endure no more. She was a slave with only a slave's faith. So she took one last risk. She put her baby boy in a basket and set him in the crocodile-infested Nile River, hoping that he would somehow drift away to safety. As it happened, the basket drifted toward the place where Pharaoh's own daughter was bathing.

By God's grace, the princess rescued and adopted the baby, named him Moses and, furthermore, hired his own real mother to nurse him for those first few years of his life. Then he was turned over to Pharaoh's daughter. Nothing more of his childhood is told.

At that point, Moses was a prince of Egypt by virtue of his adoption. However, in his first Biblical appearance as an adult, we see that he came to the rescue of a fellow Hebrew who was being beaten by an Egyptian, and the Bible indicates he knew the slave was "one of his brethren" (Exodus 2:11).

That story raises some immediate questions. First, where did this prince of Egypt learn that the Hebrew slaves were his brothers? Second, why was he willing to risk his position and even his life trying to rescue a slave?

We find an answer to the second question in Hebrews 11:24-27: "by faith...Moses looked to the reward...he endured as seeing Him who is invisible." He chose to suffer with the people of God, rather than enjoy the pleasures of sin for a season. But that brings us back to the first question. Where did Moses learn that the Hebrew slaves were the people of God? Where did he learn about "Him who is invisible" and His "rewards"?

Moses was a product of a brief, but very effective, period of home schooling. The beliefs and values and sense of identification with God's people that his parents instilled in those early years of his life shaped him forever into an arrow that God was able to use mightily for years and years to come. This was the same man who later wrote, under the inspiration of the Holy Spirit:

> Only give heed to yourself and keep your soul diligently, lest you forget the things which your eyes have seen, and lest they depart from your heart all the days of your life; but make them known to your sons and your grandsons. Remember the day you stood before the Lord your God at Horeb, when the Lord said to me, "Assemble the people to Me, that I may let them hear My words so they may learn to fear Me all the days they live on the earth, and that they may teach their children" (Deuteronomy 4:9-10).

The lesson for us—as parents of school-aged children—is that the future, including what will become of our nation tomorrow, is in our hands today. The greatest thing we may ever do in our lives is raise our children. If we will take advantage of the tremendous opportunity offered by home schooling to touch the palates of our children with Biblical Truth and with accounts of our own walk of faith with God, we can provide a generation of Christian leadership for the Church and for our Nation. They could be, as it were, a "corporate Moses"—people who look with eyes of faith to the rewards of godly obedience, rather than to fleeting pleasures of the world.

If we fulfill our calling, we can look forward to the same rewards that motivated Moses. As Moses himself wrote, "Know therefore that the Lord your God, He is God, the faithful God, who keeps His covenant and His lovingkindness to a thousandth generation with those who love Him and keep His commandments" (Deuteronomy 7:9 NASV).

Jesus said, "If anyone loves Me, he will keep My word; and My Father will love him, and We will come to him and make Our home with him" (John 14:23).

On these and many other promises from the Word of God, we can rest assured that if we take the time, effort and expense to school our children at home, they can be fully and Biblically trained, and He will supply all our needs out of His glorious riches. Our labor in the Lord will not be in vain.

And later, after we have worked ourselves out of this job, when our children stand before us as young men and women of God, we may hear God whisper to us, "Well done, good and faithful servant. You have been faithful in a few things; I will put you in charge of many things." Perhaps it will become clear to us then, that as home-school parents, we are also part of the home school "student body," as it were. We are being prepared for greater service in God's kingdom.

END NOTES

Chapter 1 — Our Children, Our Future

1. Allan Bloom, *The Closing of the American Mind* (New York: Simon and Schuster, 1987), p. 26.

2. "A Religion for a New Age," *The Humanist*, January/February, 1983.

3. Ray Sutton, *Who Owns the Family?* (Fort Worth, Texas: Dominion Press and Nashville: Thomas Nelson, 1986), p. 85.

4. Robert Lewis Dabney, *Discussions*, Volume 3 (Carlisle, Pennsylvania: Banner of Truth Trust, 1982), p. 289.

5. Ibid., pp. 278-279.

Chapter 2 — Mass-Produced Education

1. Paul C. Vitz, *Censorship: Evidence of Bias in Our Children's Textbooks* (Ann Arbor, Michigan: Servant, 1986), p. 87.

2. Ibid., pp. 87-88 (emphasis added).

3. Ibid., pp. 77-78.

4. Ray E. Ballman, *The How and Why of Home Schooling* (Westchester, Illinois: Crossway, 1987), p. 33.

5. Jonathan Kozol, *Illiterate America* (Garden City, New York: Anchor Press/Doubleday, 1985), pp. 8-9, 18.

6. William J. Bennett, *First Lessons: A Report on Elementary Education in America* (Washington, D.C.: Government Printing Office, 1986), p. 24.

7. Ibid., p. 26.

8. Tim Bovee, "If Johnny Can't Learn, Maybe Teacher Didn't," *Washington Times*, 16 July 1991, A1.

9. Rita Kramer, Ed School Follies: *The Miseducation of America's Teachers* (New York: The Free Press, 1991), 211.

10. Ibid., 209.

11. "SAT Scores Decline," *Teacher Magazine*, November/ December 1991, 21.

12. David Elkind, *The Hurried Child* (Reading, Mass.: Addison-Wesley, 1981), p. 155.

13. *Survey of NEA K-12 Teacher Members 1985* (National Education Association, Professional and Organizational Development/Research Division, 1985), p. 18.

14. "Most Teachers in Poll Cite Low Pay, Consider Quitting," Fort Worth *Star-Telegram*, November 12, 1986.

15. Verne Faust, *Self-Esteem in the Classroom* (San Diego: Thomas Paine Press, 1980), p. 41.

16. Vitz, pp. 84-85.

17. *Schools without Drugs* (Washington, D.C.: U.S. Department of Education, 1986), p. iv.

18. Ibid., p. 5.

19. Ibid.

20. Phyllis Schlafly, ed., *Child Abuse in the Classroom* (Westchester, Illinois: Crossway, 1984), pp. 50-51.

21. Ibid., p. 85.

22. Mel & Norma Gabler, *What Are They Teaching Our Children?* (Wheaton, Illinois: Victor Books, 1985), p. 66.

23. Ibid.

24. *Dolan Report Newsletter*, Vol. 1, No. 5, June, 1985, p. 1.

25. Vitz, pp. 70-71.

26. Gabler, p. 54.

27. Ibid., p. 53.

28. Schlafly, p. 113.

29. Bloom, pp. 25-26 (emphasis added).

30. Christopher J. Klicka, *The Right Choice: Home Schooling* (Gresham, Oregon: Noble Publishing Associates, 1992), p. 34.

31. Peter Brimelow, "What to do about America's Schools," *Fortune*, September 19, 1983, pp. 60-64.

32. Vitz, p. 91.

33. John W. Whitehead, *The Freedom of Religious Expression in Public Universities and High Schools*, 2nd ed. (Westchester, Illinois: Crossway, 1985), pp. 13-14.

34. R. J. Rushdoony, *The Messianic Character of American Education* (Nutley, New Jersey: The Craig Press, 1963), p. 31.

35. Ewald Plass, *What Luther Says: A Practical-in-Home Anthology for the Active Christian* (St. Louis: Concordia, 1987), p. 449.

36. Vitz, pp. 83-84.

37. Ibid., p. 84.

38. Ibid., p. 85.

39. Ibid., p. 86.

40. Ibid., p. 87.

41. Ibid., p. 88.

Chapter 3 — A Change of Scenery

1. Jay E. Adams, Back to the Blackboard (Phillipsburg, New Jersey: Presbyterian and Reformed Publishing Company, 1982), p. 138.

2. Ibid., p. 68.

Chapter 8 — Yes, But...

1. A good book that explains your legal rights and position in much more detail is *The Right Choice* by Chris Klicka.

Chapter 10 — How to Select a Curriculum

1. Vitz, p. 47.

Chapter 11 — Laboratory Experience

.   1. Various studies by Dun & Bradstreet, quoted in Inc. Magazine, The Wonderland Economy, by John Case, May Issue, 1995.

2. I recommend *The Home & Family Business Workshop*, by this author, as well as *Homemade Money*, by Barbara Braubeck, and *Master Your Money*, by Ron Blue.

Chapter 12 — Support Groups

1. Mary Pride, *The Big Book of Home Learning* (Westchester, IL: Crossway Books, 1986).

SELECT BIBLIOGRAPHY

The items marked with an * are available by mail from Christian Life Workshops. See Home School Resources for more information.

Adams, Jay E. *Back to the Blackboard*. Phillipsburg, NJ: Presbyterian & Reformed, 1982.

Aldrich, C. Joseph. *Life Style Evangelism*. Portland, OR: Multnomah Press, 1981.

Baker, Virginia Birt. *Teaching Your Children At Home*. Quitman, TX: Mrs. Virginia Birt Baker, 1984.

Ballman, Ray. *The How and Why of Home Schooling*. Westchester, IL: Crossway Books, 1995.

Barton, John, and Whitehead, John. *Schools on Fire*. Wheaton, IL: Tyndale House, 1980.

Beechick, Dr. Ruth. *A Biblical Psychology of Learning*. Denver, CO: Accent Books, 1982.

Bell, Sandra, and Wheeler, James I. *Learning Grammar Through Writing*. Cambridge, MA: Educators Publishing Service, Inc., 1984.

Bennett, William J. *First Lessons: A Report on Elementary Education*. Washington, D.C.: Government Printing Office, 1986.

Bloom, Allan. *The Closing of the American Mind*. New York: Simon and Schuster, 1987.

Blumenfeld, Samuel. *Is Public Education Necessary?* Old Greenwich, CT: Devin Adair, 1981.

—. *NEA: Trojan Horse in American Education*. Boise: Paradigm, 1984.

*Braubeck, Barbara. *Homemade Money*. White Hall, VA: Writer's Digest, 1993.

Butterworth, Bill. *The Peanut Butter Family Home School.* Old Tappan, NJ: Fleming H. Revell, 1987.

Buzzard, Lynn. *Schools: They Haven't Got A Prayer.* Elgin, IL: David C. Cook, 1982.

*Coffin, Charles. *The Story of Liberty (from the Magna Carta to Plymouth Rock).* Gainesville, FL: Maranatha Publications, 1987.

Coleman, Robert E. *The Master Plan of Evangelism.* Old Tappan, NJ: Fleming H. Revell Co., 1964.

Dobson, James. *Dare to Discipline.* Wheaton, IL: Tyndale House, 1970.

—. *The Strong-Willed Child.* Wheaton, IL: Tyndale House, 1978.

*Duffy, Cathy. *Christian Home Educators' Curriculum Manual: Elementary Grades.* Garden Grove, CA: Home Run Enterprises, 1994.

*—. *Christian Home Educators' Curriculum Manual: Junior/Senior High.* Garden Grove, CA: Home Run Enterprises, 1995.

*—. *Government Nannies: The Cradle-to-Grave Agenda of Goals 2000 & Outcome Based Education.* Gresham, OR: Noble Publishing Associates, 1995.

*—. *Home Educators' Curriculum Manual (grade by grade recommendations).* Garden Grove, CA: Home Run Enterprises, 1988.

*—. *Math Mouse Games.* Garden Grove, CA: Home Run Enterprises, 1986.

Elkind, David. *The Hurried Child.* Reading, MA: Addison-Wesley, 1981.

Engleman, Siegfried; Haddox, Phyllis; and Bruner, Elaine. *Teach Your Child To Read In 100 Easy Lessons.* New York, NY: Simon & Schuster, Inc., 1983.

*Farris, Michael P. *The Homeschooling Father.* Hamilton, VA: Michael P. Farris, 1992.

Flesch, Rudolf. *Why Johnny Can't Read and What You Can Do About It.* New York: Harper and Row, 1966.

—. *Why Johnny Still Can't Read: A New Look at the Scandal of Our Schools.* New York: Harper and Row, 1981.

Fortkamp, Frank E. *The Case Against Government Schools.* Westlake Village, CA: American Media, 1979.

*Fugate, J. Richard. *What the Bible Says About...Child Training.* Tempe, AZ: Aletheia Publishers, Inc., 1992.

—. Will Early Education Ruin Your Child? Tempe, AZ: Aletheia Division of Alpha Omega Publications, 1992.

Gabler, Mel and Norma. *What Are They Teaching Our Children?* Wheaton, IL: Victor, 1985.

Grant, George. *Bringing In the Sheaves: Transforming Poverty Into Productivity.* Atlanta: American Vision, 1985.

Hall, Robert T., and Davis, John U. *Moral Education in Theory and Practice.* Buffalo: Prometheus Books, 1975.

*Hardenbrook, Weldon M. *Missing From Action, Vanishing Manhood in America.* Nashville, TN: Nelson Publishers, 1987.

Haycock, Dr. Ruth. *Bible Truth For School Subjects.* Whittier, CA: Association of Christian Schools International, 1981.

Hefley, James C. *Are Textbooks Harming Your Children?* Milford, MI: Mott Media, 1979.

—. *Textbooks on Trial.* Wheaton, IL: Victor Books, 1977.

Henrichsen, Walter A. *How to Disciple Your Children.* Wheaton, IL: Victor Books, 1981.

Hinmon, Nelson E. *Answer to Humanistic Psychology.* Eugene, OR: Harvest House, 1980.

Hoffman, Jane. *Backyard Scientist, Series One.* Irvine, CA: Backyard Scientist.

House, Wayne, ed. *Schooling Choices.* Portland, OR: Multnomah Press, 1988. (This book includes twelve chapters on home schooling by Gregg Harris.)

Howard, Donald R. *Rebirth of Our Nation.* Lewisville, TX: Accelerated Christian Education, 1979.

Kaub, Verne P. *Communist Socialist Propaganda in American Schools.* Pittsburgh: Pittsburgh Laymen's Commission of the American Council of Christian Churches, 1967.

Kienel, Paul, ed. *The Philosophy of Christian School Education.* Whittier, CA: Western Association of Christian Schools, 1977.

*Klicka, Christopher. *The Right Choice: Home Schooling.* Gresham, OR: Noble Publishing Associates, 1995.

Kozol, Jonathan. *Illiterate America.* Garden City, NY: Anchor Press/Doubleday, 1985.

LaHaye, Tim. *The Battle for the Public Schools.* Old Tappan, NJ: Revell, 1983.

—. *Faith of Our Founding Fathers*. Brentwood, TN: Wolgemuth and Hyatt, Publishers, 1987.

Lamont, Corliss, ed. *Dialogue on John Dewey*. New York: Horizon Press, 1959.

—. *The Philosophy of Humanism*. New York: Frederick Ungar, 1965.

Lockerbie, D. Bruce. *Who Educates Your Child?* Grand Rapids, MI: Zondervan, 1981.

Marshner, Connaught Coyne. *Blackboard Tyranny*. New Rochelle, NY: Arlington House, 1978.

—. *Decent Exposure*. Franklin, TN: Legacy Communications, Publishers, 1988.

Morris, Henry M. *Education for the Real World*. San Diego: Creation-Life Publishers, 1977.

National Education Association. *Survey of NEA K-12 Teacher Members, 1985*. NEA, Professional and Organizational Development/Research Division, 1985.

Perrotta, Kevin. *Taming the TV Habit*. Ann Arbor, MI: Servant Books, 1982.

*Pride, Mary. *The Big Books of Home Learning*. Westchester, IL: Crossway, 1989.

*—. *The Way Home, Beyond Feminism, Back to Reality*. Westchester, IL: Brossway Books, 1985.

Ray, Bruce A. *Withhold Not Correction*. Phillipsburg, NJ: Presbyterian and Reformed, 1978.

Rushdoony, Rousas John. *The Messianic Character of American Education*. Nutley, NJ: Craig Press, 1979.

Schaeffer, Francis A., and Koop, C. Everett, M.D. *Whatever Happened To The Human Race?* Old Tappan, NJ: Fleming H. Revell Co., 1979.

Schlafly, Phyllis. *Child Abuse in the Classroom*. Westchester, IL: Crossway Books, 1984.

Schlossberg, Herbert, and Olasky, Marvin. *Turning Point: A Christian World-view*. Westchester, IL: Crossway Books, 1987.

Shackelford, Luanne, and White, Susan. *A Survivor's Guide to Home Schooling*. Westchester, IL: Crossway Books, 1988.

Spalding, Romalda, and Spalding, Walter T. *The Writing Road To Reading*. New York, NY: William Morrow, 1986.

United States Department of Education. *Schools Without Drugs.* Washington, D.C.: U.S. Dept. of Education, 1986.

Vitz, Paul C. *Censorship: Evidence of Bias in Our Children's Textbooks.* Ann Arbor, MI: Servant, 1986.

*Voss, Catherine *The Child's Story Bible* Grand Rapids, MI: William B.Eerdmans.

Wade, Ann. *Learning At Home: Preschool & Kindergarten.* Gresham, OR: Christian Life Workshops, 1987.

Wade, Theodore E., Jr. and others. *The Home School Manual.* Auburn, CA: Gazelle Publications, 1984.

White, Mary. *Growing Together: Building Your Family's Spiritual Life.* Colorado Springs: NavPress, 1981.

Whitehead, John W. *The Freedom of Religious Expression in Public Universities and High Schools.* 2nd ed. Westchester, IL: Crossway Books, 1985.

—, and Bird, Wendell R. *Home Education and Constitutional Liberties.* Westchester, IL: Crossway Books, 1984.

—. *Parents' Rights.* Westchester, IL: Crossway Books, 1985.

Young, Curt. *The Least of These.* Chicago: Moody Press, 1983.

RESOURCES FOR CHRISTIAN HOME SCHOOLS

The following three organizations offer important services to the Christian home-schooling community across the United States and around the world. I encourage you to write to each of the addresses for a free packet of information.

Christian Life Workshops
Gregg Harris
P.O. Box 2250
Gresham, OR 97030
1-800-225-5259

Christian Life Workshops is the organization founded and directed by this author. Through it, I design and conduct various workshops, seminars and conferences, as well as coordinating my speaking engagements with State and national organizations. CLW also publishes Home-School Favorites, our catalog of recommended home-school curriculum, books, tapes and organizers. An itinerary and catalog of materials will be mailed to you upon request.

The Home School Legal Defense Association
Atty. Michael Farris
Post Office Box 1590
Paeonian Springs, Virginia 22129

The Home School Legal Defense Association is the primary legal defense organization of the home-schooling movement. Working together with the most knowledgeable and experienced attorneys in each state, this association offers free legal services to its qualified members. "Don't stay home without it." An application and sample newsletter will be mailed upon request.

National Center for Home Education
Director, Atty. Christopher J. Klicka
P.O. Box 125
Paeonian Springs, VA 22129

The National Center for Home Education is a clearing house of information concerning all aspects of the home-school movement and a support organization to the home school leadership in each state. By monitoring both State and Federal Governments for legislation effecting home schooling, the national Center is able to alert home school leaders quickly and ward off attacks. The value of this service has been demonstrated several times. The National Center also hosts a National Leadership Conference each year which draws over 300 state home-school association directors and board members. The organization is a division of Home School Legal Defense Association, which underwrites its expenses.

National Home Education Research Institute
Dr. Brian Ray,
Western Baptist College
5000 Deer Park Drive, S.E.
Salem, OR 97301-9392

The National Home Education Research Institute (NHERI) compiles and publishes all manner of research related to home schooling, and makes this material available to organizations, schools and government agencies for their use in making better decisions regarding the education of children. Its journal, The Home School Researcher is the best source and outlet for scholarly home school statistical and social research and documentation. Dr. Ray is the unsung hero of the home-school movement. He deserves the applause and support of all home schoolers. If not for his work, many a legislature and court justice would certainly have be left with distorted, mistaken, out-of-date or undocumented information. If you are able to do so, please make NHERI a part of your monthly "mission" support. His work certainly qualifies.

Homeschooling Today
P.O. Box 1425
Melrose, FL 32666

Home Schooling Today offers a unique style with actual school activities and worksheets provided to whet your appetite for new approaches to teaching. Dedicated Christian editorial staff pursue excellence in every area of study, making this a good investment for your on-going training as a home-school instructor. Subscription information and other helpful materials will be mailed upon request.

Practical Homeschooling
Mary Pride,
P.O. Box 1250
Fenton, MO 63026-1850

Practical Home Schooling makes a distinct and valuable contribution to the home school literature. It is the publication of Mary Pride and her troupe of home-school authors and reviewers. The emphasis is on practical, with special attention to the use of the latest computer technology in preparing the next generation for high impact on the culture. Subscription information and other helpful materials will be mailed upon request.

The Teaching Home Magazine
Pat & Sue Welch
Box 20219
Portland, OR 97220

The Teaching Home magazine is an excellent Christian magazine for home-schooling families. It features high quality articles on every aspect of home schooling, all from a Christian perspective. It also hosts the most complete forum of curriculum publishers' advertising available. Subscription information and other helpful materials will be mailed upon request.

Other Home Schooling Titles From Noble Publishing

The Right Choice: Home Schooling

By Chris Klicka

This book has become the standard bearer of the Christian home-schooling movement around the world. Easy-to-read, hard-hitting, well documented, thorough, logical—these are the terms that describe the strengths of *The Right Choice*. Supplemental chapters by Gregg Harris, and foreword by D. James Kennedy make this book complete.

Item #1493—$12.95

Home Schooling Children with Special Needs

by Sharon Hensley, M.A.

Many children have special needs—from mild to severe. Home schooling works especially well for such children because it allows them to learn without the fear of social rejection. Sharon Hensley understands the challenges and offers great resources, ideas, and hope. Highly recommended! Order it for a friend.

Item #8500–$12.95

The Home School Organizer

by Gregg & Sono Harris

There are many details to keep track of in home schooling. Lesson plans have to be roughed out, resources listed, records kept—and *not* just for *legal* purposes. These records help you be more effective as a teacher. *The Home School Organizer* provides all the reproducible materials and tab sections you need to keep all the information up-to-date. Get organized and stay organized. The *Organizer* won an award for its category from *Practical Home Schooling Magazine*.

Item #1033–$34.95

Learning at Home: Preschool & Kindergarten

by Ann Ward

How would you like an early elementary curriculum that really takes advantage of the strengths of home schooling? That's what you get with the *Learning at Home* series by Ann Ward. This experienced elementary school teacher, now turned home-school mom, offers her own curriculum for preschool & kindergarten. This volume provides day-by-day plans for up to TEN subjects of study—all designed to fit into a stress-free hour & a half each day.

Item #1027–$49.95

Available Through Bookstores In Your Area
or call 1-800-225-5259

Government Nannies: The Cradle to Grave Agenda of Goals 2000 & Outcome Based Education.

by Cathy Duffy

In her important new book, *Government Nannies*, Cathy examines the devastating impact new federal education policy will have on children and families. The ramifications of Goals 2000 and outcome-based education are felt everywhere — in public schools, private schools and home schools. If you read only one book about the current educational situation, make it this one. **Item #1700–$12.95**

Choreganizers

by The Stewards

Where is the work ethic of years gone by? It's alive and well with *Choreganizers*. This unique system organizes household chores with *Chore Cards* hung neatly on individual *ChoreCharts*. *Mom Money* rewards good attitudes toward work, and once a week, *The ChoreStore* opens with an inventory of wholesome treats to buy. *Choreganizers* works amazingly well with all children ages 3 to 13. **Item #1725–$16.95**

Fun Character Builders For Kids

by Gregg & Josh Harris

Sure, kids will be kids. But all kids have to learn how to be well-behaved. The problem often lies with *parents* who swing from one mood to another so that the house rules never stay the same. With these *Rule Kits*, you'll be able to stick to a standard, and say the same things day after day. The reproducible coloring books, individual rule posters and laminated (jelly-proof) master lists work together to help children of all ages establish good habits.

The Original 21 Rules of This House
Item #1041–$10.95

Uncommon Courtesy for Kids
Item #1042–$12.95

Rules for Young Friends
Item #1036–$10.95

The Home Schooling Workshops

by Gregg Harris

Home schooling has come a long way. Now it's time to get back to the basics: the Biblical foundations. *The Home Schooling Workshops* have helped lay the foundation for over 105,000 families—those who made their initial decision in Gregg's *Basic Workshop* and others who found the resolve to continue home schooling in his *Advanced Workshop*. If you are new to home schooling, or if you are just getting a little weary of it, attend the *Home Schooling Workshop* nearest you.

Or, order the tapes of either workshop. Lay the foundation of your home school on firm Biblical principles.

Basic Tapes Item #1497–$39.95
Advanced Tapes Item #1215–$39.95

Available Through Bookstores In Your Area
or call 1-800-225-5259